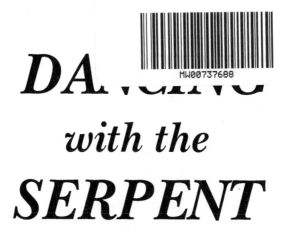

DANCING
with the
SERPENT

Diary of Madness

Patricia Anne Bloise

CasAnanda Publishing
New York   Florida

Dancing with the Serpent
Diary of Madness
© Copyright 1999 by Patricia Anne Bloise
First Edition

If the order form in the back of this book is missing, please request additional copies from your local bookstore, or write:

WaterMark Publications
PO 3366
Spring Hill, Florida 34611-3366
e mail: wtrmrk@atlantic.net

CasAnanda Publishing
Library of Congress Cataloging-in-Publication Data
Bloise, Patricia Anne
       Dancing with the serpent: diary of madness
       Patricia Anne Bloise
       p. cm. Includes Bibliographical Refernces
       Current PPD 9811

Library of Congress Catalog Card Number: 98-86659
       ISBN: 1-889131-36-9
       1. Bloise, Patricia Anne 2. Manic-Depressive persons—
       Biography 3. Kundalini I.Title
       RC464.B56A3 1998   616.89'5'092   QB197-41642

CasAnanda Publishing
POB 7207
Bayonet Point, FL 34674

I'd like to thank the following special people for their support and encouragement during the difficult task of writing this book...

my mother, who had the heart of an angel, the strength to
bear it—and for loving me in spite of myself
my Leonine son David, who never hangs up the phone
without saying , "I love you mom"
Daniel for his constant love and friendship
my brother, for playing his part so well
Dr. Mildred Harding for her editorial work
Randi Kuhne for her expertise on computer keys
Betsy Lampé at Rainbow Books for her guiding light
Mary Alice Queiros for her artistic temperament
my sweet Mary Jane who said, "I knew this would happen"
Bobbi Janson who's been there and knows what it's like
Dr. Saba, who needs no introduction
and especially Anthony Pizarro, my Peruvian warrior
who fell from heaven and landed at the right place
at the right time

For the fourteen-million Americans and their families suffering from the stigma and misunderstanding of brain disorders (formerly know as mental illness).

"If you knew how much God loves you, you would die from joy!" Brother Anadamoy — direct disciple of Paramahansa Yogananda

There is a force that dwells in the world, hidden from our view, but ever-present and waiting to be discovered. It belongs to each one of us, is sought by each one of us and eludes every one of us. No one may tell another where to look, or how to see it when it appears. It is for each an individual affair, but it is understood by all hearts.

This story is about the healing power of love. It is a story of the promise that never fails if we don´t give up hope. One that strips down to the bones of the soul with complete trust in grace.

If you find a part of yourself in these pages, if they speak to you, even if only in a whisper, then I will have met my goal. For it is only in recapturing the essence of ourselves, the love we have to share, that we achieve our essential humanity.

DANCING

with the

SERPENT

" The mind of man is capable of everything because everything is in it, all the past as well as all the future." **Joseph Conrad, Heart of Darkness**

THERE WAS THIS GULLY bird with big wings spread out over the water of Reynolds Channel. His little cylindrical body looked too small to be carrying around such big wings. I thought he looked like a baby, all grey and out of proportion. And he had teeny tiny eyes that shone like black diamonds in the sun. I could see them from where I stood in the hallway.

Gully tipped his wing and swooped down to the water's surface gliding along nearly touching it. In one motion he scooped a fish into his beak and climbed to the top of wind currents that carried him effortlessly towards the Manhattan skyline. He was late for lunch.

A bell was sounding. The bell I hated that said move along, next class, next forty-five minutes of doodles, hard wooden seats and blackboards of nonsense and inconsequence.

Students buzzed by in ragged blue jeans, tie-dyed

T-shirts, leather boots, head-bands and tatoos, cigarettes sticking out from denim pockets. They were the pot-heads, the rock and rollers, the hippies—who always wore pat-chouli oil that filled the air, making the hallway smell like Greenwich Village on Saturday night. They hid their eyes behind dark glasses, pretending not to notice they were sharing the hallway with the nerdy-jerky jocks, the sweat-men, the sneaker-wearing, muscle-pumping, ape-head jocks.

The tension was impossible to ignore. It manifested like the stench of old socks in a basketball locker room. It was the kind of tension that hangs in the air waiting to be consumed like kindling for a fire. Tension that waits and waits until it gets used up, never dissipating but always waiting, always ready for action. It came from fear and lodged itself in the hearts and minds of the students. It came from the fear of going forward, of stepping out, of leaving the familiar safety of childhood. It served a purpose then but who knew it? We could not see beyond the ends of our own noses. We were simply too young, too much inside ourselves, too much inside our differences. The pot-heads and the jocks were at war, like Godzilla meets King Kong. That's how it was, that stupid I mean.

A student had been stabbed already that spring so we had to endure the presence of these menacing looking security guards with holstered guns, who stood around from eight to three with glazed eyes and lips turned down into creepy little grins. They had these ugly round noses. They all had the same kind of noses, sort of fat and red on the ends. And they all had a little too much around the middle, making the buttons on their shirts look like they wanted to pop and fly through the air any minute. You couldn't help but feel, walking in those halls, like you were in a low-budget horror film stuck in freeze frame.

Well, let me tell you this wasn't my favorite place to be. I felt there had to be a better way to spend one's time than listening to teachers talk about stuff in text books, like the history of the American Revolution and how many soldiers died on the battlefield at blah, blah, blah... or how many layers of bedrock sonic waves pass through at minus three degrees Celsius, or about how the Chinese kill all the girl babies in China and awful stuff like that. I mean who cares? I wanted to learn what I wanted and it wasn't in books. The stuff I was interested in people didn't write about. The stuff I wanted to learn about was—well—it was the quest for enlightenment.

I was still standing there by the window when I saw my friend Larry fighting to cross the hallway against the river of students buzzing by in their change-of-class frenzy. He was wearing a cowboy hat; he always wore a cowboy hat and he was the tallest guy in the whole school, so he was easy to see. All you had to do was look for his hat. We called him LSD Larry because when you wanted it, he was the one to ask.

I watched the hat cross the streaming hallway moving in a zig-zag way stopping and starting like Pac-Man in a maze. It took five minutes for him to cross the damn hall, I swear. He came over to where I stood and towered above me. He was six-foot-three, plus two inches if you added on for his boot heels. He always wore boots, just like he always wore a hat. They were black boots with silver-tipped toes and silver buckles to match. They were pretty nice boots I thought, and besides he made an impression when he walked down the hall. His feet were heavy and slow in a John Wayne kind of way. He leaned over and whispered in my ear. "Tomorrow morning, eight-thirty at the Nook, interested?"

I looked at his face. I could never figure out his national-ity and besides he was adopted so I couldn't even tell from his name where he came from, but he looked part American Indian to me. He stood there leaning over me, smelling like that damn patchouli. His coal-black eyes were wide open and dilated, his long black hair was sticking out from his cowboy hat and he reminded me of a Halloween poster I had seen once on the back of a bus on 34th Street in Manhattan. I reached into the back pocket of my jeans, pulled out a five-dollar bill and without saying anything I handed it to him. He smiled and walked away real slow, just like in a John Wayne movie.

I stood there for a few minutes thinking about what I had just done, thinking about the quest thing, thinking about why I was doing it. I didn't need to justify my actions, I told myself. I mean, it was after all about the search for truth. Everyone did it. At least I thought everyone did it. We want to know everything when we're in high school, and even though we think we know it all already, we still believe we have it all to learn. We live in a state of constant contradiction when we're at that place in our lives. We want our independence but we're afraid, we want to be adults but we want to be kids, we want to change the world only it's really ourselves that must change... God I'm glad I'm not in high school anymore.

7

MY BROTHER WAS meditating. I could hear him. He wasn't making any noise. The only time my brother was quiet and his mouth didn't go flapping about like a flag in the wind was when he was behind his closed door. I assumed he was meditating. What else could he be doing in there so quietly?

Maybe he was a wizard and he went through a black hole into a parallel universe for a time. For all I knew he could have done that. I saw all those strange books lying around the floor of his room, and he knew how to read real well, even though I remember how when he was in the third grade he pretended to not be able to read just so he could get attention. Boy, he had everyone upset because they couldn't figure out how come he couldn't learn. They gave him all these tests in school and then had to tell Mother the bad news. "Mrs. Bloise," they said, "we're sorry to have to tell you that your son is incapable of learning to read." It was a few days after that when Mother heard him reading quietly to himself in his room.

Well, you can just imagine how angry Mother was then. Raymond always went about things the wrong way in my opinion. I never could figure out why he did the things he did anyway.

I rattled into the kitchen on a food search, found some

peanut butter and an almost ripe banana and noticed a note on the kitchen table. *Genie, Dave and Larry—tomorrow morning, 8:30 at the Nook.* And then in capitals, *I'M GONNA TELL!* I grabbed the note, crumpled it up and tossed it in the garbage.

I had the smallest room in the house, except for the bathroom. It was a little bigger than the bathroom. But it was sunny and cozy and suited me just fine. It smelled of incense and cigarettes and the east wall was done up in abstract bright colors that told a story without shyness all over the place.

Everyone that came to the house admired the wall, all of Mother's friends, especially Elmo Russ. He was a famous piano player. We had his Baby Grand in our house once. I don't know why we had it, but we took care of it for him for a while. That's when Raymond learned to play the piano. Well, he sort of learned how to play.

Sanctuary...sanctuary...sanctuary...

I was in my room, in my sanctuary and no one could bother me when I was in there. That was a commitment I made to myself and I never allowed any transgression. I tossed my school books onto the bed and eyed my wall lovingly—there was my subconscious mind spread out all over the place, and well, it didn't look too scary to me.

There was my bookcase to the right. Ah ha! Just what I'm in the mood for: *The Basic Writings of C.G. Jung.* I jumped up from the floor, grabbed the book from the shelf and stuck my face in its pages, feeling like I could absorb all that stuff by osmosis or something.

Genie was on the phone. She wanted to know what it would be like to take the stuff—she wanted to know about Alice and the rabbit hole—she wanted me to tell her it was safe, and it would be OK. I was no expert or anything you know. I mean, it was only going to be the second time but I told her she'd have fun. Yeah, we'd all have fun. What could go wrong? After all, we were friends, buddies, we always had a great time together. We were the best and besides Larry knew what he was doing, he knew about staying away from bad stuff. He had connections.

"But hey Pat," she said, "there's just one thing. I mean, well, I was wondering if you ever heard of it before?"

"Yeah, what is it Genie?" I said.

"Well, I was wondering if you ever heard of anyone getting stuck in the rabbit hole?"

"You mean like fritzed in the head? Nope. Come on Genie don't be such a putz. Loosen up girl, you're in for a high time tomorrow. Just relax and think about that beautiful beach and blueberry-cheese knishes under an umbrella

10

on the boardwalk. OK? See ya tomorrow morning at eight-thirty."

I went to sleep that night with nightmares about a rabbit in a cowboy hat and black silver-tipped boots chasing me up and down the boardwalk on a Baby Grand with a sack of blueberry-cheese knishes and a copy of Jung's basic writings in his pocket.

A BIRD WAS CHIRPING in a tree outside my window. Sunlight felt warm on my cheek. I heard the morning news coming from the kitchen. The man on the radio said, "It's currently seventy with a high of eighty degrees coming at us folks. What a great Thursday we have in store for us! Are you ready?" Such enthusiasm was disgusting before seven in the morning.

I stretched my neck turning my head to look at my cat clock with its big round plastic eyes that moved back and forth left to right, all the while swishing its tail in a predictable metronomic rhythm. Cat said: 6:58.

I had just enough time to shower and grab a cup of coffee. I made my way into the kitchen mumbling words of greeting to Mother, who was seated at the small round breakfast table.

"Hi mom," I said, stumbling across the room. I walked

over to the refrigerator, opened the door, took out a quart of milk, put it on the table and sat down to wait for the coffee to finish perking.

Mother looked up from her breakfast of fruit and crackers. She always ate fruit and crackers in the morning, usually bananas and oranges or pineapple, or sometimes she ate these funny little Jewish cookies that were shaped like stars with the points taken off.

"Good morning daughter. Did you sleep well?" Her words blended with a Ritz.

"OK, I guess. Where's the paper?"

"Didn't come yet sweetie," she said. She got up from the table to pour cream into her cup. "Oh, yes. Can you please see if your brother is up yet? Thanks."

I went to see the bear, it was still sleeping. "He's in la la land," I yelled across the house walking towards the bathroom. "I'm off to shower. Save me a cup of java, Mama."

LARRY DAVE AND I stood in front of the Cozy Nook at eight-thirty that Thursday morning waiting for Genie to show up. We just stood there together not saying much, each of us inside our own expectations, inside our own heads, anticipating what was before us, making ourselves real small inside so we could fit down the rabbit hole.

I kept looking in the direction of Genie's house to see if she was coming, till there she was walking down the block, real slow like a snail in molasses. It looked to me like her feet were not sure of the way to go and I figured she was having second thoughts about the whole thing.

Larry handed me a little piece of white paper. It was about half an inch square with a blob of brown material in the center. I popped it in my mouth and it dissolved almost immediately. It was tasteless, odorless, unidentifiable, mysterious. I felt the inside of my mouth with the tip of my tongue. I couldn't feel anything. My tongue had gone instantly numb.

Genie joined us and stood next to me smiling hello. She wasn't in the mood for talking, I could tell. Without a word Larry handed her the dot, and she hesitated for a moment just looking at the thing in her hand, not saying anything.

I thought she was acting sort of strange and I was already starting to wonder about the day, wondering if we were going to regret our choices later on. She just kept staring at her hand, like she was waiting for something magical to happen there. Finally after forever passed by she popped it in her mouth.

13

THE BEACH WAS CHILLY. Springtime morning chilly, like when you can't wait for summertime to come so you pretend it's already the season for bare backs and tanning lotion.

The rising sun already about thirty degrees above the horizon warmed the air currents bringing to life a wind dance that played over the water. Ocean waves tumbled and turned reaching into the air in perpetual motion. The life pulse of the sea could be read on the shore in the rhythm of the waves.

Not a soul could be seen along the stretch of beach as far as your eyes could see. Except for a few brave surfers in wet suits trying to catch a wave here or there, no one was around.

The four of us walked across the empty beach down to the water's edge and decided to climb out onto the jetties. You had to be real careful out on those rocks because they were so damn slippery, being covered the way they were with this slimy green moss that was always wet from the spray coming off the waves. You had to be real careful that you didn't slip down in between those monster rocks. Boy, you'd really be in a fix if you did that.

It's pretty interesting how those giant boulders got put there on the sand like that, all neat and even in rows up and down the length of the beach. Elephants put them there. Yeah, back in the 1920's or some time around there some-one had this great idea about getting a bunch of elephants to push these giant rocks all around into these neat and tidy rows about five-hundred feet apart up and down the water's edge to act as breakers for the waves. Those elephants did a really nice job too, a really nice job I think—but of course that's only my opinion. I don't know anything much about that sort of thing.

I sat down on the flattest spot I could find and stared out over the water. I watched the waves breaking along the end of the jetties ten feet in front of me. A fine spray misted the air getting my hair wet. I sat there quietly for a while thinking of the last time I visited that spot on the rocks. I had taken LSD then too. That was the first time, first time down the hole.

Only it hadn't been a hole. It was more like a different dimension. Light bent in funny ways there. People walked backwards and disappeared through walls. Funny colored lights materialized in thin air, becoming shapes, then melting away into nothing. Trees talked, flowers hummed, electric wires made noise. There were magnetic fields everywhere that pulled against your skin teaching you things you would never believe if you had not seen it, felt it,

15

learned it, through your own senses. Time expanded and lost its meaning. The sunset became the sunrise and yesterday and today lost their separation. All the moments of all the tomorrows one might ever hope to know, became known and felt in the bones, in the blood, in the beating of the heart.

I remember after a while I had gotten used to all that and then there I was standing there looking out over the sea. The wind was blowing pretty good that day and I thought to myself—everything. I want to know everything. Miss Know It All wanted to know everything. Big mistake to ask the universe a favor like that. But I did.

I asked the sky, the wind, the clouds, and the ocean to tell me all their secrets. The universe whispered back at me, "It's only an illusion. There is nothing to learn, nowhere to go. Remember the laughing Buddha..."

"Are you going to the Hendrix concert, Dave?"

Larry's voice brought me back to the group. He loved Jimmy Hendrix and he was always looking around for someone to go to concerts with.

Dave pulled a cigarette from his shirt pocket. "Don't know about next week Larry. Probably try for the Jersey concert in August. Heard it's a great show."

"Hey if you do it, pass by one for me, I don't mind

crossing the river, OK?"

"Yeah, no problem, Larry. I'll get what I can get and we'll do it, man."

I wondered why Dave didn't ask me or Genie along. Probably some kind of male thing I guessed. I didn't want to make a big deal about it even if it did seem rude.

I thought about that Dave guy for a while. He really seemed different. I mean, take for instance his clothes. He always dressed in black: turtleneck, jeans, boots, rims of glasses—black. Then there was his disposition: sometimes animated, joking around and stuff like that, but sometimes he was too damn quiet. He had a good sense of humor too, but it was subtle, you had to pay attention. He was very smart, you could tell just by looking at him how smart he was, honor classes at school and all that. One of those types that didn't even study or hardly open a book. He only liked to read Ray Bradbury and Isaac Asimov. He was really into that science fiction stuff.

Genie pulled a lighter from her pocket, a cigarette from her pack, and tried to light the thing, but it was too windy. She decided she needed some exercise and jumped down off the jetties and started running like mad along the shore. I jumped down right behind her, my feet sinking three inches into the sand. I loved that feeling—the feeling of sand between my toes. It always made me feel so connected to the earth, so grounded.

Fifteen feet in front of us, sand pipers ran frantically along the receding water's edge, searching with their razor sharp vision for hermit crabs hiding just beneath the surface. Each wave of the out going tide brought a piper closer to its next meal as a small measure of sand was removed with the movement of the water. Eventually the little crabs would be revealed and consumed by their destiny.

We're just like the little crabs hiding under the sand, I thought. Each wave comes along like a dream in the night bringing us closer and closer to our truth, but all of a sudden —there's the piper!

The four of us walked along the shore playing tag with the waves in the sun, happy in our rebelliousness, happy to be there on that beautiful beach.

I noticed a mild euphoria and changes in my perception. The blue sky was bluer, the warm sun was warmer, the ocean sounds were louder. Sea gulls flew above the jetties in a graceful dance that described wind patterns blowing off the waves. The birds, the wind and the ocean were one being, existing together, for each other. There was complete harmony. Time became meaningless as patterns of perception blended together and I became the gulls, I became the wind and the ocean. For an endless moment I was free.

"Hey, let's go sit under the boardwalk for a while!" Larry was motioning towards the shade. By now it was ten o'clock and people were slowly appearing on the beach, dragging along the kinds of stuff people always drag along with them when they go to the beach: umbrellas, beach chairs, frisbees, radios, volley balls, little kids, pails and shovels for the little kids, snacks, drinks, sandwiches, a dog or two.

We made our way towards the boardwalk. Sand moved under my toes. I could feel each grain like tiny needles in the soles of my feet. My legs felt like rubber bands kind of springy and wobbly.

We sat together on the damp sand—no one had remembered to bring a blanket. Larry suddenly started to laugh out loud, but he didn't let us in on it.

"Say, Genie," I said, "did you finish your English paper yesterday?"

She shook her head no. Her hair looked blue, then yellow. Her eyes flashed like suns going nova. I could see through her. Right through her body I could see the waves turning on the shore. She was really an angel, that had to be why I could see through her. She wasn't a real human after all. Boy, wasn't I lucky to have such a friend. I felt honored.

"I'm always late for Randolph's class," she said. "I must

have a block about writers of the 20th century. It was a lousy paper anyway. It's just as well I do it over." Genie pulled another cigarette from her pocket, and Larry lit it for her. The lit end looked like a bright red light bulb.

"Hey, look at that cloud!" Larry was pointing out over the ocean. "It looks like a pyramid made out of some kind of irridescent crystal. Wow, that's awesome!"

Each of us became lost in our own experience of the clouds, of the wind, of the moment. I thought I heard the sound of a woman's laughter. It was the sound of the wind playing under the boardwalk.

I could smell the scent of the ocean. It reminded me of something very ancient, something I could not name. The sun was melting in the sky, dripping ribbons of yellow light across the horizon. The breeze blew them into giant petals of color. The horizon began to wave and wobble into an arch making the world circular. Life was a circle. I was a circle. My body began to turn in a circular motion. The world turned upside down. The world became yellow light.

I lay down in the sand, closed my eyes, and my body disappeared. I had no beginning and no end. I was expanding out and away from myself. All my edges were dissolving into nothing. Everything became nothing until there was only the sound of the ocean in the distance, and yellow light.

"Let's see about something to drink, guys. I'm getting kinda thirsty," Genie said. She got up and brushed sand from her clothes. So we all got up and brushed sand from our clothes.

"Say Genie, so what do you think about this stuff anyway?" I asked as I walked out into the sunlight.

"Gee, I don't know," she said, putting on her sun glasses.

"I guess it's like being in a dream only I'm awake. And everything in this dream is spontaneous and free. Anything can be created and the world just keeps enlarging itself." She started rubbing suntan lotion all over her arms and legs.

"Sounds like a pretty good description to me. What do you say Larry?" I noticed that funny little grin on his face.

"Well Pat, I say it sounds like we're in control, so we must be OK." We laughed together at the good fun of it all.

We made our way towards the ramp that would take us onto the boardwalk; there were concession stands up there that sold food to beach goers during the warm months. One of the best places to go for a bite was this great spot called Izzy's Knishes. They had the best knishes in the world: cheese and fruit; blueberry, strawberry, pineapple. No one else on the planet had anything like them.

I thought about the nightmare just then, about that stupid rabbit in a cowboy hat with a sack of blueberry-cheese knishes on top of a piano chasing me up and down the boardwalk. I never did figure out what that dream was about.

THE BOARDWALK WAS crowded for a weekday morning. There were mothers with small children in strollers, and mothers with older children testing their independence by running across the boardwalk zig-zagging their way through the bicycle path, as their mothers yelled at them for safety's sake. I saw elderly folks sitting in the sun out of the wind engaging in casual friendly conversation.

"How was breakfast?"

"Did your son visit on Sunday?"

"Did you hear about Martha's husband? It's such a shame."

Genie and I walked over to Izzy's while Larry and Dave headed for a hamburger stand.

"Hey Genie, you know what I think?" I said it real quiet, like I was going to tell her the world's best kept secret. She looked at me. Her pupils were wide open and dilated even in the light.

"I know, you're going to tell me you like Dave, right?"

"Get off! How'd ya know? It's not that obvious is it?"

"Hey, I've known you since the third grade, remember?

Besides, don't you know you can't hide stuff from best friends?"

We stood in line and waited our turn, but when it was time to order, I had no appetite, not even for a knish, so I just bought a soda. Genie asked for a cup of water.

The guys were sitting at a wooden table near the hamburger stand, so Genie and I walked over and sat down without saying anything. We all just sat there looking out at the beach, looking out across the wide blue ocean, and I couldn't help but notice how the sunlight played against the expanse of white sand, sand that stretched out in opposite directions east to west as far as I could see, sand that was clean and fine and beautiful and too often taken for granted by those who didn't stop to appreciate it like we were doing then.

I breathed in the clean salt air, I breathed in my life trying to suck it up inside myself, trying to fill in the blanks like a hangman's game—watch out! fill in the letters before your head gets in a noose.

We decided to walk on the boardwalk with no destination or thought about what to do next. As we made our way along, I noticed David was especially quiet, so I asked him how he was doing.

"Hey Dave, how are you feeling? What do you think of

this stuff anyway?" Silver light danced in his hair. I saw alien worlds alive in his eyes. I figured he had Asimov and Bradbury in his head taking notes for the next best sci-fi adventure.

"I'm fine, just taking it all in. Say, Larry, can I bum a butt from you? I have to get a pack."

Larry handed David a cigarette and he lit it without losing his stride. Such a mysterious one, I thought. It was his quiet and deliberate mindset that observed and was unaffected by what it took in. Still waters run deep; that statement was made for David.

"Hey, you guys," Larry said, "how about we head up to Park Avenue, maybe we can see if Pig-Man Mike is back from class."

Pig-Man was this really cool friend, who had a sort of extraordinary talent in art and science. He liked to put together light shows at a place called the Fillmore East.

We all had had enough of the beach and the boardwalk so we headed towards the center of town. The four of us were just walking along cutting school, thinking we were cool because we were doing what we wanted. We were making a statement being rebellious and all that, walking along heading towards Park Avenue.

Long Beach has a Park Avenue because in the 1920's and

1930's it was a place where rich people would go for the summertime, leaving New York City and places like that. And when they made up the street signs in Long Beach they figured they should have a place called Park Avenue so the rich people would feel at home. Well, I don't really know if that's true. I just made it up, but it's probably some stupid reason like that.

Well anyway, so there we were, Larry and Genie and Dave and me. I was minding my own business. Just walking along Magnolia Boulevard, and this impression came to me from somewhere, only a vague sense of awareness really, of being so open, so vulnerable, so small. Well I just said the words, "I feel open to attack," just like that. I said them to no one in particular, just for the hell of it. I didn't even know why I said them, and I didn't think anything of it. But David did.

It took a while for us to notice the change in him. Something happened to him that day somewhere along the way. He stopped talking and retreated into himself into a place none of us could imagine. He just walked around with us, sort of there but not there. We were afraid to press him for conversation. We became quiet ourselves, feeling his need for silence. There was an odd sort of vulnerability that had become exposed. We all felt it. There was an awareness in my mind then, of the fragility of the human psyche underneath its outer layer. Underneath that exterior part we display to each other, to the world, another self is quietly hiding. It's the piece of ourselves we never allow out except in our dreams.

David had entered that place that day and it was frightening for him to be there. It was scary to us too, seeing him like that, so quiet and unreachable. None of us knew what was happening to him. Hours passed but he didn't speak. What could we do? None of us knew about "bad trips," none of us knew how it could get, or what to expect.

We just went along in a kind of silent limbo trying to be supportive of our friend. The day passed us by, and we never did get to see Pig-Man Mike.

We hung out just walking around the streets of Long Beach waiting for our friend to come back to us. Finally by eight o'clock that evening things were beginning to lighten up as the effects of the LSD were wearing off. We decided it was time to call it a day. When we were saying our goodbyes David finally spoke to me.

"Can I call you when I get home?" His eyes were pools of dark fear. I felt his sense of urgency.

"Of course you can call me," I said. I was grateful to hear him speak after eight hours of silence.

When I got home, Mother was sitting in the livingroom. I didn't say any thing but went straight to my room. Within twenty minutes the phone rang. It was David.

"You read my mind!" he said, in frantic monotone syllables. There was a heaviness on the line and I wasn't getting the message.

"Do you remember when you said those words, open to attack"? "Well you read my mind!"

It was telepathy! David was talking about telepathy! I knew the significance this would have for him. I knew instinctively that this was profound for him. I didn't even know how I knew it, but I did. We talked until the sun came up.

We became inseparable. We shared ideas, philosophy, science fiction, fantasies. David had a fertile imagination and a keen intelligence that was also deep and broad. But he carried within himself a deep cynicism.

There were things that bothered David—things he wasn't willing to share—things too difficult to talk about. He was a private person even at that young age. But I came to understand later on how vital our early relationships are. David suffered from a terrible grief, a profound sense of disconnectedness. He had witnessed the death of his father at five years of age, and his young mind had not been able to understand the tearing away of his father from him. He suffered the loss of himself in the loss of his father, and his burden of sadness had been overwhelming.

Time passed. We smoked pot, went to concerts, lit candles and incense and listened to the Moody Blues. We were young people in love, trying to find completion in each other, because we felt so incomplete. It seemed as if the missing parts of our souls could be found somewhere beyond the boundry of ourselves.

We began to meditate together. We would sit cross-legged on the floor of David's bedroom holding hands. One day we decided to do this after taking LSD.

It was evening, the room was dark. A candle's timid glow cast dancing shadows against the walls. Incense was burning. Music was playing in the background. David and I sat in the middle of the floor with our legs crossed and hands held together. It was comfortable sitting like that.

I faded into the music in a relaxed way. I had no knowledge of meditation technique, I only knew that it was something I wanted to do, so I trusted my instincts, and I played it by ear.

Minutes passed: ten, fifteen, twenty, I'm not sure. At first there was only an awareness of peace and serenity and the heaviness of my body on the outside, but of a lightness within, as if I could move to an interior part in the middle, almost as if I had two bodies. I felt a sensation in the center of my forehead. I saw a light there beginning to form. It was a white light, very soft at first, not strong. It seemed to have a magnetic pull to it, and I felt its field. My body was very relaxed, my heart rate had slowed down, and my breathing was no longer noticeable to me. My whole attention had become fixed on that white light

Suddenly I felt myself moving. I was moving through a tunnel. The tunnel was very long, but at the end was that white light. The tunnel did not frighten me and the light did not frighten me, but suddenly I was in a panic because I felt my body being pulled through that tunnel at an incredible speed. I didn't have time to think about what was happening. The sense of speed was beyond my comprehension. I knew that if I let myself go into that white light there was no coming back. I jerked my hands away from David's. My eyes flew open—my heart was pounding. David was sitting with his eyes closed. A moment later he was looking at me. We never spoke about this experience and we never meditated again.

IN THE SUMMER OF '69 WE went to Woodstock where everyone ran around naked, listened to loud music and took drugs. I had a wonderful time except I didn't run around naked or take drugs because I knew by then that taking drugs wasn't going to answer any questions for me. It just made things more confusing after a while. But I loved the atmosphere of it all, just like everyone else. It was a kind of phenomenon I guess, Woodstock I mean. And all of us together like that, so many of us in one spot, well, the vibrations were pretty strong.

David and I talked about joining the Pig Farmers. They were a group of free spirits that had taken to living off the land on a farm somewhere in the Midwest. But we were too bound by convention and unwilling to take that kind of risk. We chose to stay caught up in the boundary of the familiar because we lacked the courage to step out into the unknown. It was something I would come to regret later on for David's sake.

School continued to be a drag and became more and more boring to me, as my desire to learn a broader knowledge grew. I simply could not relate to high school material. I wanted to know about truth, about what could not be perceived with the limited instruments of the human mind. I was Miss Know It All standing on the jetties asking the universe to tell me all her secrets.

If the universe wasn't going to tell, then I thought I could use my ESP. I knew I had all the answers already anyway, all I had to do was dive deep and find them. The only problem was, I never learned how to dive. But what the heck? I could learn as I went. How bad could it get? How confusing could one tiny universe of knowledge be?

This was my soul quest, my mission. I was frustrated with learning, and I was disillusioned with school. This prompted me to make a major decision. I would leave high school.

I WAS IN THE LIVINGROOM. It was a Saturday morning when I made my announcement to Mother as she sat there sorting through some papers.

"Mom, I want to drop out of school," I said.

Mother looked surprised. No words came from her mouth, she just sat there looking at me.

"I can't stand going to school with armed guards in the halls. Everybody hates everybody, they're always fighting and I don't want to be there!"

Mother was quiet for what seemed to be a long time. Finally she said to me, "You may leave school against my wishes, but if you are not going to go to school, you must go to work."

OK, I said to myself, so I'll go to work.

Monday morning I was in the principal's office. Mrs. Schwartz was the secretary. "I decided to drop out," I said abruptly. Schwartz looked at me and shook her head.

"You'll be back," she said with certainty. She gave me a bunch of papers. "Here, take these home and have your parents fill them out," she said, still shaking her head.

I took the papers and left the office. I went straight to my locker, pulled out my stuff and said goodbye to high school. It was that simple.

I walked home, dropped off my books and headed downtown. Long Beach had a Headstart program, and that seemed like a good place to begin. I marched myself into the office, filled out a job application and one hour later I was employed as a teacher's assistant.

I'M NOT GOING TO tell you the details of my life after high school while I was working as a teacher's assistant and all that because I really don't feel like going into it right now. But I have to tell you the important stuff, like David and I got married and had a baby and everything was sort of too much for us—and we separated—and well, I got depressed about the whole thing and had it really rough for a while. Well, we both had it rough for a while.

Donna, from high school, who I hardly knew at all came

by one day. She had this woman with her, the woman's name was Jana. Now I don't know why Donna brought someone I didn't know at all to my house—except I guess Donna thought that the stranger and I could be friends because we both had little kids the same age—which is actually what happened. We got to be friends after a while.

But anyway, that first day this woman Jana stood outside for a while talking about this and that and I could see right away she was a really interesting person. I guess I'd have to say she had a kind of charisma. She seemed young and old at the same time. Her face looked young but her body seemed sort of matronly, slightly rounded in the shoulders, giving a tired appearance to her frame. What was most noticeable to me though was her calmness, her quiet and graceful demeanor. She had a sort of confidence about her. That was what first set Jana apart from other people in my mind. I found her so interesting to talk to I invited her over for tea the following week. That's when my education in metaphysics began.

Jana read tarot cards, used crystals and pendulums, felt objects with her hands and knew things about the people they belonged to. She went into trances all of a sudden and said funny things I didn't understand. The first time she did that she scared me to death. Sometimes she played the zither and sang like an angel. She was New Age she said. I didn't know too much about all that myself, it was 1973 and I didn't even know we were having a New Age then, or why we needed a New Age, but it sure looked like it was doing Jana a world of good.

But that New Age stuff wasn't really what Jana was about. What Jana was about is much more important than that, and even though I saw it back then I didn't really understand it yet. I was still too busy looking around at nonsense.

Jana and her husband were poor. Very poor. They lived in a crowded one bedroom basement apartment with a couple of dogs and not much else. They were simple and easy going people. Nothing seemed to bother Jana. She was always pleasant, always happy, and held this inner calmness that was extraordinary.

She and her husband gave to one another an honoring affection and respect. They were possessed by some magic, some incredible inner knowing that was visible to anyone who looked. They lived beyond the constraints of our society, unbound and unbridled by the should's and have-to's of most people caught up in the maze.

Jana's inner vision was a reflection of a superior way of life and it seemed to me that if everyone in the world was like Jana, then the world would be a great place to be. She became a kind of mentor to me, teaching me about things I wanted to know. She talked a lot about Christ, about his missing years. How did she know I wondered? History is an unreliable source, it has been rewritten countless times. But Jana wasn't talking about history, she was talking about knowledge, the things she spoke about were part of her knowing, part of who she was.

The boundaries of understanding began to stretch for me. I began to appreciate more and more that reality is determined by one's interpretation of events and personal expectations. I began to think about history and that it might be meaningless. History presupposes that time flows in linear progression. That idea no longer made sense to me as my understanding of time was beginning to change. My mind seemed to be opening up to new ways of thinking. Ideas formed of themselves, images and symbols came to me from nowhere. Information was pouring into my mind in an unbelievable way. The universal mind was beginning to speak to me.

My relationship with Jana continued for some months, until suddenly she and her family disappeared from my life as quickly as they had entered it, when one day I went to their apartment and they were gone. I never found out where they went or why they went away.

I became interested in occult thinking. I read about Buddhism. Herman Hesse's *Siddhartha.* India. I became fascinated with India. I was mostly interested in the traditional ideas, the ancient wisdom that predated Christianity, because I reasoned, ancient knowledge was the source and I wanted to know the purpose of it all and my reason for being. Depressed teenagers need answers. I know I'm repeating myself, but well, I'm trying to make a point....

AND THEN IT BEGAN the first time. The energy came from somewhere, and took me over—body, mind and soul. It was there all of a sudden, showing itself at first as an insatiable appetite for music, and drawing pads and pencils, oil and canvass—sketches in abstract design, sketches of any limb or part of my anatomy that could be kept still and poised so it could feed my need to express this new part, this new element. I was tireless, without need of food. The flesh began to disappear from my body and my clothes began to hang on me. I talked fast and thought fast. I had fast ideas and places to go. I drove to the airport at three in the morning to watch the planes landing, wondering who was coming in on those wings and where they were coming from—so many people, so many people. My mind was making pictures. Someone or something was filling my mind with symbols and abstract ideas. Not words came, not language as I knew it, but a geometry and landscape of shape and form. My mind was a river of knowledge flowing through a channel of eternity. There was no time, only the ever-present now that expanded forever and ever. So much to do. I wrote a poem and a song and a story. I played the piano. I lost my appetite, my sense of time, my sleep. Day ran into day, the sun was up and down. It meant nothing but whether or not to put on a light.

After three weeks without sleep, I was deep into it. My subconscious mind refused to be ignored. It was as if someone had taken a barrel filled with endless pieces of a giant puzzle and scattered them out all over the ground, and that someone said, "These are the parts of your life. Good luck putting it back together." And I could hear the universe. She was laughing at me.

I REMEMBER STANDING IN my livingroom, it was early in the morning as the sun was coming up. I started to spin like a top. I didn't lose my balance or get dizzy. I just remember spinning.

Later on that day Mother came to see me. She took one look at me and at my apartment, which was a terribly disorganized mess. Mother called my brother. They decided I needed help.

Even though I had lost the connection between my inner and outer experience, even though I was lost in a world that was making no sense, I will never forget the date. It was October 6, 1973, the day of the Yom Kippur War, and the boundaries of time had been completely obliterated. My mind was afloat in a sea of information that was making no sense. And I had learned the answer to Genie's question: yes indeed—one really can get stuck down the rabbit hole.

IT WAS NIGHT TIME and I was outside Mother's house. I wasn't doing anything wrong, just taking a walk. The street was quiet—no traffic around, or people either. I was wearing my pajamas. My pink silk pajamas as a matter of fact. Big deal, huh? Well what was the big deal? So what if I was walking around in my pajamas?

Inside the house my brother Raymond and my mother were developing their conspiracy. They were in there talking about me. I could hear them saying the words as if I was sitting right there in the living room.

I walked down a dark street twenty feet from Kerrigan Canal. The moon cast its silvery grey beams on the surface of the water. The reflection of light slipped back and forth left to right, in hollowed out pockets of water.

The words Mother was speaking came into my head: "Something is seriously wrong with your sister, I don't know what's gotten into her but look at her out there walking. Is she on drugs? Oh dear God, what am I going to do with her? Ray, I want you to take her to that doctor of yours, you know the one in that place. Yes, take her there tomorrow."

I didn't want to hear it. I covered my ears with my hands to stop the words but it didn't help, because my hands were made of paper. I held them out to Mr. Moon to see if he could write on them to make them real, to make them useful, but he just shone on with that smiling face of his adding insult and ridicule to my request. I stared out over the water.

The door to Mother's house opened. Raymond came outside to get me. I ran behind a giant hydrangea bush and hid there until he went away. After a while I went back to the house and climbed through my bedroom window.

At three in the morning your heart beats really loud. Every thing else is so quiet, that's why. I tried to listen to its rhythm so I could fall asleep but it didn't work. I tried counting sheep, I tried hot milk, I tried a glass of wine. I even tried sleeping pills. I was going to die because my heart was going to wear out.

I got out of bed, went to the desk, and pulled out the drawing pad and pencils I'd bought two weeks earlier. I sat down and propped my left foot up on the desk. I liked the way it looked, it had a kind of elegant shape to it—nice toes and all that. In five minutes I had managed to draw a likeness of the form in front of me. I smiled to myself—not bad I thought. I ripped the paper from the pad and placed it on the growing pile of sketches on the floor.

I sat down in the chair facing the window and stared out the glass at Mr. Moon and thought about what it was going to be like when I was dead. I thought about it until the sun came up.

I was in the kitchen sitting at the table sorting jellybeans. The green ones did not belong. One by one I tossed them into the sink but some of them fell onto the floor and rolled into the grout lines between the ceramic tiles. They made a pretty pattern here and there so I added some red jelly beans, then some yellow. I ate some and I tossed some more till the floor was covered and all the beans were gone. It just seemed like the thing to do

I STARED AT THE funny looking man in the long white coat while my brother was talking. He was talking too fast. Well, he was nervous of course, he was nervous telling that man terrible lies about me. He can't help it he's what you call a psychopathic liar. My brother kept looking over at me then back at that man all the while waving his hands around like a lunatic. He is very emotional, especially when he's lying.

The man in the white coat, that Dr. Allyson person, was listening real close to my brother, as he went on and on about the things I had been doing, like staying up all night, playing music too loud, walking around the street in my pajamas and throwing jellybeans all over the floor. That Allyson person didn't seem too impressed, as he sat there listening and writing stuff down on a yellow piece of paper.

I didn't know why I had to be in there with them just listening to it. They could have let me sit in the hall or maybe go out and get a cup of coffee. They were really boring me. I was just about to get up and leave when Raymond said to me, "Hey Patti, tell him who you are."

Well, that was a pretty stupid thing for Raymond to say after all the stuff that was going on in the world. It was Yom Kippur, Israel was at war and everybody thought the world was coming to an end. Well, some people thought the world was coming to an end. So I just looked at that Dr. Allyson person and I told him I was the Virgin Mary—and don't ask me how come I thought such a thing—I can't tell you.

An hour later Raymond was gone and I was officially mad, crazy, non compos mentis, off my rocker, deranged, potty, pixilated, berserk, buggy, cracked in the head, batty, daft, loopy.

I decided to go to the bathroom. I went into a large narrow room covered completely in white tile. It looked the part, real hospital like I mean. The room gave me the creeps. I went over to the mirror and stared at the face in the glass. I saw beautiful rosy cheeks and paper-white skin that was too delicate looking to be real, with eyes that were fully open and dilated, eyes that were circles of black without brown color in the irises. There seemed to be a cloud of energy around that figure in the mirror, some odd sort of aura. I asked her who she was. She didn't speak. I waited for her to answer, but she didn't. She gave me the creeps too, so I left.

Outside of the ladies' room, the hallway turned right then left in a zig-zag way. Then it became a dead end. It seemed as if I was in a maze—how the heck could anyone figure out their way around? I knew I had to be real careful because this was a dangerous place. There was a war going on. The enemy was everywhere. He was everybody.

I REALLY WANT TO tell you about Gloria. About how my heart stopped short and I almost dropped dead right there on the spot and could hardly believe my eyes. I kept blinking at her thinking that maybe she was an apparition or something like a hallucination.

She shuffled past me, it looked like in slow motion and I noticed how thin she was, how she didn't stand erect but kind of leaned over to one side, how her head tilted in the opposite direction attempting some kind of compensatory balancing act. Her right elbow was permanently bent like it had rigor mortis or something, and the only function of that elbow was to support a claw-like hand that offered a continuous smoke to her toothless mouth. Well, it was a smoke when someone was kind enough to replace the butt in her hand with a fresh stick. She didn't feel the blisters on her fingers and couldn't care less how many times a butt had burned into the tips of them. She had long curling fingernails, fu-man-chu style, and filthy dirty besides. Her face had one eye instead of two, and the socket was all shrunken up like a dried prune. Her hair was matted and she smelled like urine really bad.

The worst part about meeting Gloria though was hearing her chanting. Well, I guess I can call it that because I can't think of a better word right now. But anyway, there she was as she shuffled along, repeating this squeaky hissy sounding rhythm, "Gloria's the snake, sssnnnaaake in the garden, Gloria's the snake in the Garden of Eden," and then she'd make a funny little clucking sound under her tongue.

44

I wanted to drop dead from the hell of it, but I just started to cry like a baby right there. Allyson's nurse came over to stick me with a needle.

"My name is Nancy (big smile, shiny teeth). Dr. Allyson ordered this medication for you. Which side do you prefer?" Fluid dripped from the end of the syringe. It looked like maple syrup. I let her poke me on my left side.

THE ROOM WAS SPINNING. I was in the dormitory and it was spinning. No, I was riding on a carousel of beds that didn't bob up and down but went round and round on a stationary plane. There were six rows with eight beds in each row, going around and around. I had the second bed from the wall in the second row on the right side of the room. I managed to land on a bed... I was out.

A woman was screaming. I was having a nightmare. Tell it to go away Pat, I thought. I listened for the source of the sound, it was coming from far away. I was standing in a wide open field surrounded by trees. A fierce wind was blowing through the branches, bending them near to the ground, scraping the face of the earth with their graceful digging. They were dancing trees—what a lovely nightmare I am having, I thought. But there was something else, something else in the field, something that wasn't pretty.

There were dead bodies everywhere. I didn't want to look.

I opened my eyes, it was night time, there was very little light. I didn't know where I was. Nothing looked familiar. I was in a strange bed, in strange clothes, made of stiff cotton that smelled of bleach. I lay there for a moment just listening. That woman was still screaming. I felt a sense of panic, there was something very wrong here. Who was she and why was she screaming like that? Maybe she had been captured in the war? Maybe she was being taken prisoner? I slipped my legs over the edge of the bed and felt for the floor. I stepped out across the room groping in the dark and found a locker. I wasn't sure if I should look in it. I felt dizzy and very thirsty, my mouth felt like it had cotton in it. I opened the locker. It had a robe in it, and since that was what I had been looking for I guessed it must have been mine, so I put it on.

I headed towards the hallway. I could see the screaming woman. She was strapped down on a gurney—her arms and legs were thrashing about. Nurses and aides were standing around her, holding her down. There was an IV pole at the head of the gurney. Oh my God, I thought, they're trying to kill her! She's been captured and they're trying to kill her! Panic swept through me. I knew my life was in danger. I had to be very careful—watch what I said and did. Had to be real careful who I talked to, didn't want to wind up like that screaming woman. I just stood there. I felt helpless. There was nothing I could do for her, nothing I could do to help that poor woman. In a few minutes she calmed down. She was quiet and still. They did it! I thought. And as I watched them taking her away I knew I'd never see that screaming woman again.

Boy I was really scared now. Things just kept getting more and more confusing. I was tired and wanted to go back to that hard strange bed but I wanted to know what was going on in that terrible place.

I made my way into the day room. There were patients there watching television. One of the aides (his name was Pete) was handing out stuff to eat: coffee and doughnuts. Hey, not too bad, I thought. I was hungry for the first time in weeks. I wasn't sure I should trust Pete but everyone else seemed to be eating so I guessed it was all right.

"Hi, what's your name?" Pete handed me a doughnut.

"Pat." I stared at the floor.

"Here's a cup of coffee. If you need anything just ask me or one of the other aides, OK ?"

I went over to the group and sat down on a couch in front of an ancient black and white television that was suspended from iron braces bolted to the ceiling. There were seven

47

patients sitting around watching television and munching away on doughnuts and coffee.

There was Debbie, who was probably in her early twenties. She had long blonde hair, and big green eyes that flashed with fear when she got angry. She was sort of chubby and seemed kind of tough, like if she got upset she could really get on with it. The funny thing about Debbie was she also thought she was the Virgin Mary. We didn't like each other too well, and I kept my distance from her. Sitting alone on a chair near the nursing station was Old Soul, a young Jewish man with straight black shoulder-length hair that fell gently around his face. His beard was full and long. He had beautiful calm green eyes, and pale anemic-looking skin. He carried his small trim frame with an air of dignity and purpose, looking like a young Rabbi who had strayed onto the wrong path.

One fellow thought he was Napoleon. He was a young man about twenty-five who had a creepy face that told all about the misfortunes of life. He seemed agitated all the time. He was tall and strong and capable of causing a major problem for the staff if he got upset.

There was an older man who thought he was a gargoyle, another man who was very depressed, and sat staring at the floor most of the time, a woman who had lost her husband

48

and could not recover, another who hated her mother and wanted to kill her.

These were seven strangers, whom I had never seen before and would never see again but who were now temporarily my peers in Wonderland. All of a sudden while I sat there the music to Rock Around The Clock began playing in my head.

"SHOWER TIME EVERYONE!" A young woman stood in the center of the day room yelling into the air. She was very pretty, with long dark hair twisted up on top of a round oriental face. She was surprisingly tall for a women, but slightly built with delicate bones. She wore blue jeans and a cotton T-shirt like all the other aides I had seen, and no jewelry or accessories of any kind. Only a key chain with three keys hung from her side pocket.

Old Soul walked across the room heading towards a pair of old rusty iron gates that led to the outside. He was dressed in a black short-sleeved shirt that was missing all its buttons, a pair of white denim jeans, a purple velveteen cowboy hat with a black feather sticking out of it, and black sandals with heavy rubber soles that looked like pieces of automobile tires. I wondered if he would notice the cold October air or if he was like the snake-woman who didn't feel the burns on

49

her fingers. He crossed in front of me and headed outside with measured steps that were slow and deliberate. He was in no hurry. He knew the routine well and he knew his place in the society of crazies. I went to my locker and got my things together to take a shower.

Bathing with the women of building 22 was a community affair. I remember thinking to myself that first evening I might be in there with the snake-woman and that idea—well, you can imagine it didn't make me too happy. As I made my way into the shower area, I struggled to comprehend what peculiar derailment of purpose had brought me to this place. I was a little confused yes, but did I belong here? I mean, after all, anybody who hadn't slept in three weeks would get a little confused, wouldn't they?

Inside the shower area I saw some of the women being assisted by staff. Patients who could accept help without screaming, kicking and biting were lucky to get in there each evening. I found a spot in the corner and turned on the water. At least it was good and hot. I let the water stream down my body, trying to wash away the reality of the place. How could it be that in this life where men had reached out to the stars, walked on the moon and created giant cities of technology with information highways, this scene from the middle ages was unfolding before me? I tried to keep my focus close and limited, to not see the naked bodies of the women in front of me. They didn't look too good. It wasn't a question of being overweight, although that was part of it. What was difficult to accept was the incredible distortion of proportion and form. Bent frames with hunched shoulders, extended arms, hands and fingers, stiffly and ineptly drawing circles of soap and water in aimless fashion across stretches of skin whose integrity had been compromised to a degree unimaginable by those of us with healthy tissue. Scars, scabs, ulcerations, rashes, hives, scabies, crabs, all manner of plague had run their course and taken their toll. Flesh hung loosely on bent bones, while toothpick legs seemingly incapable of supporting the abundant poundage of upper bodies stood before me. It was impossible for some to reach as far as the knee, certainly not below to get feet clean or pick up a bar of soap as it slipped to the floor. None of these women were past the age of sixty years. My sensitivities won out. I decided that the next evening I would make sure to be finished showering by eight.

I WAS SITTING ON my bed. Impressions of the day swam in my mind. I thought about my boy, who was just two years old. It was good fortune for him and for me that he had a caring grandmother. Because of her efforts during this difficult time he was well taken care of.

I closed my eyes and tried to stop an endless procession of thoughts: the events of the past few weeks, of the day, of the people in the place. The effects of the Thorazine took over. I fell into a drugged sleep.

I was adrift on a raft on a lake of calm water. Moonlight shining across the mirror image of night, reflected on the face of the lake. In the distance there was a sound unidentifiable, and foreign to my ears. I held my breath and listened. A groaning, from deep within living tissue, raw and savage, haunted the pocket of lake. Above me hung the black velvet canopy of eternity like some giant orifice of mystery, beckoning me to journey deep into it if I dare. Faithful sentinel of the night, Brother Moon, his bright center burning like ice, kept his mark.

The haunting sound began in rhythm, joined by the song of jungle birds squawking in shrill voices. A cacophony of sound began to vibrate molecules of water and air. A gentle heat engulfed me. Heat increasing—light flashed yellow—red—the black canopy of night revealed itself— the veil was lifted... there was nothing then... but the magic sound in the mouth of God... and one tiny heart beat...

VOICES WERE SINGING IN the air. It was six o'clock in

the morning, and the sun had not yet risen, but we were expected to get up. Two aides came into the dormitory with quick steps flicking on lights and turning down beds as they went.

"Wake up time everyone! Let's go! Let's go!" They yelled in tandem.

I struggled to bring my mind into focus, to crawl out from beneath the undertow of Thorazine sleep. I sat up slowly, the room was spinning again. My head felt like it would explode. I tried to get out of bed, but changed my mind, and fell back onto the hard pillow. That thing is like a rock, it's no wonder I have a headache, I thought.

A woman was climbing out of the bed next to me. I could see she was very frail and tiny. She had long straight grey hair that was braided and fell with a kind of heaviness down the length of her small frame. She turned and looked at me.

"New huh?"

I nodded my head, yes.

"My name is Kandi. Pleased to meet you." She turned away and headed towards the bathroom.

I made a second attempt to rouse myself from the bed. A little better, I thought. A little better. I got up slowly, being careful not to move too quickly, telling myself that with a little aspirin and a nice sensible cup of coffee I would be as good as new.

It was seven o'clock. Nurse Nancy was out on the floor with her medication cart calling out names. One by one the patients approached the cart while Nurse Nancy looked in her big blue book, made a mark with her pen and dispensed a pill or two. Then she handed out a little cup of juice and looked under everyone's tongue to be sure everything went down. When it was my turn I was handed two round brown pills, with "300" on them. I looked at her.

"Thorazine," she said to me.

"Can I have some aspirin, please?"

She shook her head no."Only if the doctor orders it," she said.

I looked at her face again. She smiled and returned to her work. Total control, I thought. They have total control.

I sat on a hard wooden bench in the dining hall and leaned my elbows on the picnic table in front of me. My behind was sore. Patients were eating breakfast. They looked like cardboard figures posed in silence. They kept their faces looking forward, avoiding eye contact with neighbors or staff. I felt like I was in a Woody Allen movie.

Old Soul sat to my left at the next table. He looked pale that morning, even more pale than he did the day before, when I first saw him. Looking up from his plate for a moment he caught my eye. He smiled faintly and returned to the business of breakfast. I have to talk with him, I thought. I have to talk to someone here before I lose it.

The cardboard figures continued to eat in silence. I kept looking around for some sign of life, some sign that would make an affirmation to me, so I would know I had not really died and gone to hell. Maybe that's what happened I thought, maybe I was dead but didn't know it. Maybe I died in my sleep with the trees in the field and just didn't realize it.

I WAS IN THE DAY ROOM. Twelve patients sat there, still doing the cardboard routine. They just sat on the maroon vinyl in their cardboard way with their cardboard faces. The seven o'clock dose of Thorazine was starting to hit me. I felt light headed, the muscles in my back felt tight, my fingers were stiff. Chemical straight jackets. That's what's wrong with everyone here I realized suddenly. That was the reason for the overwhelming inertia.

Old Soul walked across the room. He was heading for the gates that led to the outside. I got up quickly and followed him. He sensed I was there and slowed his steps so that I could reach his side.

"Mind if I join you?" I asked.

"My pleasure," came the reply.

Outside the air was clean and fresh. The radiant sun felt wonderfully warm on my face. Yellow light danced against greenery, reflecting itself in shadowy mists under leaves of oak and maple. Tall blades of rye and bluegrass stuck up needle like, millions upon millions of them pointing their way into the cool October air, happy to grow there quilting the sleepy earth as she prepared for her quiet season to come. October is the best I told myself. The outside never looked so good. A feeling of peace slipped in for a moment.

"Got a cigarette?" I asked my new friend.

Old Soul reached inside his pocket and fished out a broken promise of a smoke. It was hand rolled. I gratefully accepted. "So tell me," I said, "how long have you been here?"

"Six months." He searched his other pocket and pulled out another cigarette. "I have no place to go. My family refuses to let me go home and they can't discharge me without a place to live."

I looked at him. No words came to me to speak.

"This place is Mordoor," he said waving his arm in the air. He pointed in the direction of a very large red-brick building standing about five-hundred feet in front of us. It had been built to house the mentally ill during the 1920's and boasted twelve floors of barred windows and broken glass, and heaven only knows what stories were left behind haunting those rooms. The building was badly in need of repair, and was one of many structures on the grounds that had been abandoned years before.

"I see what you mean about Mordoor. This place gives me the creeps. So what's your name?"

"David," he said.

I looked at him for a moment, appreciating the special meaning that name held for me.

"People tell me I'm an Old Soul." He brushed his long hair away from his face.

I held my hand out to him. He had a gentle but firm grip. "My name is Pat." I said.

David turned away, his voice trailing. "None of this is real you know. It's merely the dance, the play of Maya. She has mesmerized us with her charms and we are her slaves, addicted to her romance. Even though at times she is cruel and vicious, still we adore her, because we don't know any better."

I followed behind once again in slow steps. Maya? I said to myself. The word sounds were strange in my ears.

Old Soul turned to look at me. "Maya," he said. "The veil of illusion. It's what one perceives through the delusion of his own ego. There is no individual self—there is only

God."

We walked in silence. I became lost in my thoughts. I was confused. Nothing was making sense again. Maya, Maya—she's a liar. Maya, Maya—pants on fire. Maya, Maya—gonna get you higher. Thoughts came in sing-song and nonsense. Bing Crosby chews bubblegum underneath the gum-drop tree. Maya darling, send this over to Crosby for me. Maya, Maya—give and take—eat more steak— Maya, Maya—the cosmic liar.

David stopped walking and turned to me with his Rabbi face. "Don't get caught up in it Pat. Keep on guard, watch out or master ego will destroy you."

My feet turned to lead. A sudden tiredness came over me as I spoke to David. "It's beautiful outside, but I think I'd better go back in for a while." He smiled at me and continued walking.

I WAS IN THE EMPTY day room sitting on a couch. The television was on without the sound. A lady wearing a green dress and green heels was standing beside a green car. Her mouth moved up and down while she gestured over the thing indicating its graceful form and shape. It was a Thunderbird, a green Thunderbird. I watched her mouth moving without words and tried to see inside it, to see if maybe her tongue was green too but her mouth wasn't big enough.

I thought about Old Soul. What the heck was a master ego anyway and this thing called Maya? I wondered what kind of books he was reading. Pete the aide came over. "Good morning Pat," he said. "Can you please come with me? Dr. Allyson would like to see you now."

I followed Pete to Dr. Allyson's office. He was sitting at his desk writing in a folder. "Please sit down, Patricia," he said motioning to a brown leather chair beside his desk. I sat down in the chair feeling anxious.

"So tell me, how are you feeling today?"

"OK."

"Do you know what day it is, Patricia?"

I just looked at him without saying anything.

"Do you know where you are?"

"Yes," I said. "This is Mordoor. "

Dr. Allyson wrote a little while in the folder on his desk. I looked at the wall behind his head. It had seven pieces of paper mounted and framed in plain black wooden squares, forming a checkerboard pattern against a grey wall. Seven was my lucky number, and I guessed that was why I had Dr. Allyson to be my shrink.

A nurse knocked on the door. She had long red hair and

freckles all over her face and long skinny legs that stuck out from a tight white skirt. She had on red nail polish and she was wearing high heels. I tried to look in her mouth while Dr. Allyson exchanged a few words with her.

"I will be right back, Patricia," he said as he left the room. I sat there trying to remember if I had ever seen nurses that wore tight white skirts and high heels. I noticed Dr. Allyson had left my folder open on his desk. I reached across to look at it. In the upper left corner of the inside cover printed in neat even letters were the words: *Paranoid Schizophrenic with Delusions of Grandeur.* I didn't know what that meant but I knew I didn't like the way it sounded. Allyson came back in. He sat down and continued writing in the folder.

"OK Patricia. I'll see you tomorrow," he said. He didn't lift his eyes from the paper.

I WAS IN THE DAY ROOM again. "We have group at eleven o'clock in the lounge. John and Tracy are running it this morning." Pete made a notation on the clipboard he always carried around with him, and then walked towards the nursing station.

Debbie came into the room and walked towards the gates leading to the outside. She crossed in front of me with quick steps, her feet moved in rhythm but her arms remained motionless at her side. She was dressed in a dark blue sweatsuit, her head was covered by a hood attached to a matching jacket. I watched as she passed through the gates making the sign of the cross and bending her right knee ever so slightly in a gesture of respect to her guardians. The music to Rock Around The Clock started playing in my head again.

I WAS READING A pamphlet in the visitors' lounge that informed me I was in a famous place. Pilgrim State covered almost two thousand acres, and was a model psychiatric facility in the late 1920's. In its early years Pilgrim had actually been a city all by itself and was completely self-sufficient. It was home to as many as thirteen-thousand patients with a staff of twenty-five hundred to keep the city going, and was the largest hospital of its kind in the world. It had its own power company, water supply, police department, fire department, post office, cemetery, farm land, laundry service, amusement hall, athletic field and green houses. It was at that time the institution that set the standard and showed the way for hospitals that were to come after it.

Now the once famous model hospital was run down, and decaying slowly like some gigantic dinosaur that was too

stupid to give in and yield itself completely to the new way
of things. Institutions were a thing of the past. I put the
pamphlet in the garbage.

I was outside. I was outside because I wanted to find Old
Soul to talk to him some more. I spotted him walking about
thirty yards in front of me, heading towards the commissary.
I began walking in his direction.

The commissary was a place where patients could go to
buy cigarettes, candy and soda. They moved in and out
from there in a constant stream. There was simply nothing
else to do and nowhere else to go. Maybe today I can buy a
pack of cigarettes, I thought.

I caught up to Old Soul and matched my pace to his
stride. We walked in silence for a few moments. I noticed a
stiffness in my back and my neck, and as I walked along I
felt slightly off balance. The muscles on the right side of my
face were in some kind of spasm. I noticed David's pace
was slowing. He seemed fatigued and I wondered why he
had difficulty walking.

He picked up my thoughts. "I have pleurisy," he said. He
pressed his hand against his chest, then held it out showing
me the tips of his fingers. They looked blue. He searched
inside his pocket with his blue-tipped fingers, pulled out
two cigarettes and handed one to me. He lit my cigarette,

then his own.

"Are you going to the eleven o'clock group, David?"

He looked at me with incredulous eyes. "I do not attend those groups," he said.

"Why not?" I asked, surprised at his reaction.

He studied the sky for a moment then pulled out a pair of sunglasses. "Going to groups will not help my problems," he said. "I know where the source of my trouble lies. It's my attachment to my experiences of the world that cause my problems. My desires for personal gratification, and my memories, these are things that must be challenged. Here is where my work is to be done."

I sensed anger and frustration in his voice and didn't understand what he was talking about. "I don't understand you David. What do you mean attachment to your experiences and memories cause your problems?"

"My issues are karmic, just like everyone's," he said.

David searched his left pocket. He pulled out a little piece of paper, handed it to me, then he continued."People think karma means being punished for sins but that's not really true. Karma is memory. It means being held prisoner by one's own memory. Part of this delusion comes from the illusion of time. All time is happening at once and it's simply our memory of it all we're experiencing. Our consciousness is simply caught in a time lag. In other words, the future is already the past. People don't see into the future. They see the ever-present that's always happening. When the individual finally realizes this, then he may become free of it if he chooses."

I looked at the little piece of paper: *It is the man who creates his karma, for it is the product of his own thought* —DHAMMAPADA. I handed the paper back to David.

"How did you learn about all of this stuff ?" I asked.

"It's just a process of growth," he said. "We all go through it one way or another, we all learn it sooner or later."

I walked along trying to understand, trying to make sense, trying to find places in my brain where those words would fit. I wondered about memory and about time all happening at once.

"Say, David, what do you think about people remembering past lives? I mean, you know how some people say they can remember their past lives when they get hypnotized. Is that what it is? They just see all time happening at once?"

David pulled the zipper of his jacket up to his chin and stuffed his free hand in his pocket. "Sometimes people can access memory through DNA. It's in the genes, in the genetic material where there exists a living record of our race."

"A living record, of the whole race? You mean the whole species? That's a pretty interesting idea David, but what about the memory part? How does that explain people remembering past lives?"

David dragged down on his cigarette. "It's our genetic memory. Every cell in the human body has retained in its DNA the entire history of life on this planet, and sometimes people can access part of that memory, even specific parts of that memory, but of course accuracy of memory can be questionable. A person may access specific lifetime memory and erroneously think it belongs to him. In that case he is merely the observer of the memory, not the person who lived that life. The really amazing part though is that we all have the same DNA and therefore potentially the same memory. Our experiences differ only because everyone has a different complement of activating bits of DNA. We're really just clones of each other at different angles."

I stopped walking and turned towards Old Soul. He kept walking. He didn't pause, he didn't slow his pace, he just continued on his way to the commissary.

I WAS SITTING ON a metal folding chair. I was in room

number 8, group therapy room number 8. There were four other patients sitting quietly waiting for group to start: Debbie the Virgin, the gargoyle man, the woman who lost her husband, her name was Marion, and Gloria. We sat there in silence. I was glad the room was quiet. I needed to assimilate, to associate, to connect this idea of karma-memory to my life.

I looked at Debbie. Was it possible that she and I were two totally unrelated individuals in the same place at the same time sharing the same memory? David used the word 'delusion' and I knew Allyson would agree with him, but where did David's definition begin and Allyson's end? Was it possible that Old Soul's explanation was the right one? At least he had an explanation. He certainly had more to say on the subject than Allyson did. I stared into space. I stared into the silence.

Tracy and John came into the room. They pulled chairs to the center and asked us to do the same with our own chairs. In a moment a circle was formed. John asked us to wait a few minutes to see if more people would come.

The young man who thought he was Napoleon, or maybe he was the man who was stuck in the memory of Napoleon, came into the room, sat down between two empty seats and began tapping his fingers together in a nervous fashion, up and down in the air in front of his face. After a few moments he stopped. I noticed a slight tick on the left side of his face and a large scar below his cheekbone on the same side. He didn't smell very good.

John began. "I think we can start group now. My name is John and I'm going to be running this group today along with my co-worker Tracy. I encourage everyone to participate because that's how you can begin to gain some degree of control over your life, by first deciding to take responsibility for being here and by giving yourself the power to make decisions about what you want to do while you're here. I would like to begin by having the members of the group introduce themselves. Let's start over here." John pointed in my direction.

One by one we went around our half circle, calling out our names. Gloria didn't want to say hers and jumped up out of her chair and ran from the room.

"Who would like to tell me a little bit about why they're here?" John looked at us, and waited for someone to speak.

Suddenly Napoleon shouted at him, "They're commos and commies and they put you here cause they think they're better than anyone else. And they think you stink!"

"Who thinks that?" John asked him.

"The ones that don't talk!"

"Who are the ones that don't talk?"

"The ones with the golden eyes and I don't want to talk to you anymore buster!"

"It's OK. You don't have to talk with us anymore."

The group was quiet, no one spoke after that. John tried to get the other man in the group to speak, the one who thought he was a gargoyle, but he wouldn't open his mouth. Debbie wouldn't either, she just sat there staring at Tracy's shoes the whole time. Marion, the woman who had lost her husband, wouldn't speak either. Everyone was shut up inside a little box, stuck inside their own head, without words to release them. It was like the grey matter was stuck and along with it the spirit was stuck too. After twenty minutes of getting nowhere John gave in and ended it.

I STOOD IN LINE in the dining room, hoping to catch sight of Old Soul. The room was already full with patients waiting to be served.

While I stood there I noticed a peculiar sensation in my spine—something was moving. It was no longer an ordinary spine with stationary vertebrae that moved and flexed to support the twisting and turning of head, trunk and limbs— that housed spinal fluid and nerves that came together in pockets of tissue, glands and organs of life. What was formerly straight and even had become a twisted mass of current, slithering up and down the length of my back in a serpentine motion. It's the damn drugs, I told myself. It's my energy fighting with the drugs—psychic energy that wants to express itself but is being pushed down, locked in by the drugs.

I saw Old Soul make his way into the room and take his place in the lunch line at the opposite end of the serving area. At least I will be able to sit with him I thought.

I got my tray and took a seat at a table close to the other line. There were three people sitting there already, sitting in their cardboard way behind their walls of separation, behind walls of impenetrable defense against their own fear. Worlds of fear and guilt and shame, these were inner realities projected outside the self and onto others, any other being outside the self would do. It was an act of preservation but in the act of saving the self from fear, the self became isolated, alone, cut off.

Old Soul saw me sitting at the table. He walked over and sat down next to me on the bench-like seat that would accommodate five or maybe six people.

"Hi David," I said. "I'm glad you came to have lunch. It's nice to have someone to talk with, especially after that group."

"Today is pancake day. Sometimes I skip lunch but not on pancake day." Old Soul gestured toward the gastronomic delights.

Once a month the kitchen would prepare a pancake smorgasbord offering different kinds of pancakes, waffles and crepes along with a variety of fruit and toppings. It was a little bit different and fun for everyone. A rare experience for the inmates of building 22. "How was your group?" Old Soul pushed his hair behind his ears.

I thought about the lack of communication. "It seems that the people here cannot communicate. But I wonder why they have so much trouble expressing themselves? It's almost like a kind of autism or something."

David poured blueberry syrup over his waffles. "You know how when children are young they think everything in the world revolves around themselves? Well, if there is too much childhood trauma, too much childhood stress, then as the child learns about the world the brain learns how to perceive through those emotions." David cut his waffles into small pieces. "The brain grows along with the body and keeps developing throughout life. It doesn't really stop developing." David powdered his waffles in sugar. "However, when this person becomes an adult his body has grown an organ that doesn't function properly, it has grown an organ that perceives through the world of the wounded egocentric child self. The childhood traumas become as large as the life of the individual." A piece of a drenched and powered waffle found its way into his mouth.

"So how does the person get fixed?" I asked.

It took a moment for the waffle to go down. "By really learning how to love himself and by taking care of himself. By learning how to recapture his natural spirit of joy. Medication is fine, but it only affects the body. It doesn't help with the inner struggle, it doesn't help the wounded spirit of the individual. No matter how much medication we take, we still have our own demons to tame, don't we?"

I noticed the three people sitting at the table were staring at David, but they didn't say anything. I waited a moment before I asked my question, hoping they might join the conversation. They remained silent.

"You're talking about healing of the spirit, not a cure of the body, not a physical cure, right?"

"Yes, I'm talking about spiritual healing and that doesn't necessarily mean physical healing. There are plenty of people with unhealthy bodies, whose lives are filled with love and joy. And there are others who are blessed with wonderfully healthy bodies but whose spirits are crying out for something more."

"But then David, how does someone have a spiritual healing when we don't even know what we are in relation to it? Most people don't bother to think about that part of themselves until they're in a crisis. I don't see how a thing like that can be possible."

A playful smile crossed his face. His eyes looked like emeralds in the light. "It's only possible if the individual is willing to learn how to love himself unconditionally, the way God does. That's the way of spirit—to rise above human judgment—that's what's meant by 'ascend into heaven.' Heaven exists right here and now when we learn to love ourselves unconditionally."

"That's all very fascinating David. Why didn't you become a teacher or something?"

He smiled at me. "Karma," he said.

There he goes again with that word, I thought. On the way back to building 22 I noticed the sky looked overcast. I thought it might rain.

NURSE NANCY STOOD in the center of the day room next to her medication cart, punching pills from cardboard sheets. She was preparing her midday medication rounds. She saw me come into the room and engaged me eyeball to eyeball and, with her pointer finger crooked under her nose like the crotchety old witch in Sleeping Beauty, called me over to her.

"Here Patricia, the doctor ordered this for you."

"What is it?" I asked suspiciously.

"Cogentin. It's for your stiffness."

Then I understood the tightness I was feeling in my body, the change of flexibility and motion. The serpentine current in my spine. It was happening in my brain, not my body.

I went to get a sweater. I was going for a walk. I changed my mind and decided to take a nap. I changed my mind again and decided I would rather sit in the visitors' lounge.

I was in there rudely listening to the conversation between Debbie and her visitor, her mother. I could understand in a few short moments what a pitiful relationship she had.

"Look at your shirt! Don't you have anything cleaner to put on than that? Didn't I tell you I would buy you some clothes? Why don't you let me buy you some clothes? Why do you deliberately try to undo all the nice things I have done for you? You are so ungrateful sometimes, Debbie. I don't even know why I come here."

Poor Debbie was red in the face and getting redder by the moment, but that didn't stop her mother. I wondered if I could wrap her mother up into a small square package and put her in the garbage can.

I went to the dormitory for a nap. There were no sheets or blankets on any of the beds. All the pillows were gone too. Someone had come into this large room full of people's beds and removed all the bed clothes—just removed everything leaving the room naked and sterile. They didn't want anyone in bed during the day. This was their modus operandi, this was how they did it. They just made you hate the beds, that's all. It was simple. They knew I was going to take a nap so they went in there and did that awful thing to the beds.

I SAT ON A BIG over-stuffed chair in the day room looking at a magazine. All the words were in French. It was a French magazine about French food. Looking at it made me feel hungry, so I stuck it under the cushion.

Old Soul came into the room. He asked me to take a walk. I went to get a sweater from my locker in the dormitory. I noticed all the beds: every one of them was done up neat as a pin. Somebody in this place knows how to make beds really fast, I told myself.

He was waiting for me by the tall iron gates that led to the grounds, the place where Debbie always paused to genuflect and make the sign of the cross.

We walked along the little path which led us outside to the rear of building 22. The overcast sky I had seen only a little while ago was gone and now the sky was sunny and bright and wonderful looking. I couldn't help but notice how acute my perception of light had become. It seemed as if all of nature had acquired a golden glow. It was clearly the angle of the sun's rays as they struck against the trees and bushes and everything my eyes could see. Colors were extremely bright, I had never seen such intense shading. Everything had a kind of ethereal quality, an almost supernatural look. It was as if some magic had taken over my senses and being outside in that glorious light brought an experience of euphoria to me, one that cannot be fully described in words. It was extraordinary and I remember thinking that I must have been suddenly transported to heaven on invisible wings.

"Let's sit on the grass by that big oak over there." Old Soul pointed off to his right. We went over to the tree and sat down under branches growing barren from the season's change. I kept absorbing that extraordinary light.

Old Soul took a folded piece of paper out of his jacket pocket and handed it to me. I opened it up and read:

in the mirror—large eyes

heaven is them
dimensions of another world
the muffin man—psychobiotic feet
don't touch the ground
six hundred milligrams of thorazine
what's your game?
dr. john the night tripper
the machine of your cerebrum
needs more anti-freeze
what level of consciousness have they chosen?
they think that what they choose is real
there's more than one way to skin a cat
knock knock, who's there?
take a guess I double dare
sticks and stones can't break your bones
it's only an illusion
he who laughs last laughs best
my friend said that his name is Buddha

I finished reading and handed the paper back to Old Soul.
I tried to understand the meaning of that piece of writing but
I couldn't begin to imagine what it was talking about. I just
looked at him. Who is he? I asked myself. Who is he really,
and why is he in my life?

"So, Pat. Do you like it?" He asked.

"Well, David, I cannot say I understand it. It's extremely confusing just like my whole life lately. If you don't mind I'd rather not talk about it."

"I'm sorry. I guess it is a strange bit of whimsy."

"I don't think I would classify that as whimsy David," I said leaning into the tree.

"Yeah, I suppose you're right. The fellow who wrote it was a jazz musician who was also a Buddhist. He even went to Tibet when he was studying his religion. He's had a lot of trouble finding his way."

"Just like all of us, huh?" I smiled at him and as I looked at his face it was clear we understood one another.

" Hey Pat," he said. "What do you say we go back inside, it's getting chilly out here." We stood up together. Old Soul offered me his arm. We walked back to building 22 side by side, friend by friend. An awareness had opened up between us, a friendship of understanding. A Robert Heinlein word came into my mind. Grock. It was good.

I WAS LYING DOWN on my hospital bed looking up at the ceiling. Fluorescent lights ran across the area in parallel rows about four feet apart. The ceiling claimed forty bulbs in ten rows, which could be turned on in sections to conserve energy. The room was pretty bright, because all the lights were on. I went over to the wall switch and turned off all the lights but the ones at the far end of the room.

I returned to my bed and lay down again. The room was much softer looking without all those lights on. I closed my eyes and began to allow myself to relax into my thoughts. Feelings came to the surface, not really ideas but emotions that were hard to name. They were vague impressions from some time long gone. There was a sense of aloneness, a sense of sorrow, a sense of emptiness. I thought about that writing David showed me. Strange was inadequate to describe its verse: *What level of consciousness have they chosen? They think that what they choose is real. There's more than one way to skin a cat.* That made a connection for me. I understood that idea pretty well. It spoke to me about individual experience and that each of us determines our own reality, according to our own perceptions. Each of us is stuck in our own projection of ourselves into the world, the world David called Maya. And it's only a memory anyway. Maya Maya she's a liar. Maya Maya pants on fire. Maya Maya the cosmic sire.

Thoughts tumbled around, endless thoughts, endless psychic mumbo jumbo—the monkey mind, that unruly creature that makes us spin our wheels had hold of me and

I was out of control. My restless monkey mind was out of control.

THE PRETTY ORIENTAL aide came into the dormitory. She said her name was Sharon, and that it was time for supper. She escorted me out to the day room. When I got there I saw that most of the inmates were waiting to go to dinner. Before we were allowed to go, everyone had to get medication. The nurse was having a difficult time with Napoleon. He didn't want to cooperate. The nurse was trying to reason with him but he would have no part of it. The more the nurse tried to convince Napoleon he needed to take his medication, the more agitated he became.

Kandi, the little woman with the long braided hair, went over to him and whispered something in his ear. His mood changed immediately. He took his pills. I looked at Kandi. She smiled at me and went to the gates to wait for our escorts. Napoleon followed right behind her.

I walked over to the rest of the group realizing I wasn't going to be called by the nurse. That was quite all right with me. I was beginning to resent the medication because of the side effects. For some reason I thought of Gloria. I wondered what had happened to her. I hadn't seen her since group. I figured she was probably hiding out somewhere smoking her cigarette butt down to her fingertips, and chanting to herself in the language of her private world.

WE MADE OUR WAY again, into the dining hall. Old Soul was nowhere to be found. I wound up sitting with Kandi and the young woman who hated her mother and wanted to kill her. Her name was Paula and she talked to herself. The whole time she ate her dinner she talked to herself about her mother and why she hated her.

"Mommy will come back later baby, don't worry, don't worry, don't cry baby, don't cry." She repeated this over and over as she ate her dinner. Sounded like she had an abandonment issue to deal with. She did not respond to us and could not or would not be distracted from her focus on her internal dialogue. It was almost like some kind of weird mantra. She seemed to be in another world, like all of us stuck inside our own little worlds.

We are all the same, I told myself. Just variations on a theme. It was like someone took a story line and then said, you and you, and you, this is your dialogue, let's see how you play it. And we played it. Everyone of us in our own way playing the same story using the same lines with our own twist, our own interpretation.

"So Pat, what do you think of this place so far?"

I looked at Kandi's face. She had soft brown eyes that had a kind of dreamy look to them. There was nothing hostile or unfriendly about her.

"I don't know why I'm here. I don't think I belong here, and it would be nice if someone would tell me what's going on."

"Did you see your doctor?"

"Yeah, I saw him earlier but he didn't tell me anything."

"Listen Pat, let me give you some advice. If you need to know something, ask. Don't assume they will tell you anything because they won't. You have to ask questions. Don't be afraid. You have a right to know. It's your life."

"Gee, thanks Kandi, I appreciate it."

"No problem. If I can help you in anyway I will. I have been at this game for a while. Who's your doctor?"

"Dr. Allyson."

"He's my doctor too. I like him. You'll probably get to go home for a visit in the first three weeks of your stay. He likes to see how people handle going home right away."

"First three weeks? How long am I going to be here?"

"Most people stay about four months. Some people stay longer and some not that long. It all depends on discharge arrangements."

Four months! I couldn't believe it. That seemed like an

eternity to me. I thought about my boy. I felt angry.
Thoughts started to race—angry thoughts—hopeless
thoughts. I was angry at the doctor, at the hospital, at my
mother, at my brother. I was angry because I had no control,
no say about anything. I had been stripped of everything, of
my very self. No one had the right to do that to me. Who did
they think they were anyway? What gave them the right to
put me here? I was furious. Just wait until I get out of this
place, boy am I going to show them! I was so angry. I had
never felt that way in my life. Tears came to my eyes. Kandi
sensed my feelings. "Don't worry Pat," she said. "It will all
work out. You'll see."

I looked at Kandi. She had such beautiful eyes it was
hard to be upset when you looked at her. In a moment I felt
calmer. I finished my dinner and excused myself from the
table. I walked back to the main building, thinking about the
questions I would ask Dr. Allyson the following day. I knew
Kandi's advice was worthwhile. It made perfect sense to me.

When I got back inside the building Pete called me over
by the nursing station. I wasn't as lucky as I thought earlier.
The nurse was preparing an injection for me. She came out
of the fishbowl with the Thorazine.

"OK Patricia. Let's do your right side this time."

"Why do I have to have an injection, why can't I just take

this stuff orally?"

"You will be on oral only, beginning tomorrow. Doctor wanted you to have three doses by injection in the beginning of your therapy and this is the third one."

I was glad I asked. Kandi was right, you had to ask questions."Why is my mouth so dry, and why am I so stiff?"

She handed me a little white pill. "This will help with the stiffness. You need to drink a lot of water, that will help you also."

I was handed four ounces of juice. I swallowed the pill. "Thank you."

"You're welcome," she said. She took the cup and didn't check under my tongue.

I turned and walked away still feeling angry at everyone and everything. What made me really angry was I couldn't figure out what had happened to me. How had I earned the diagnosis Dr. Allyson had given me? How did he make that diagnosis? He knew nothing about me. What did it all mean anyway? I bet even the doctor didn't know what was going on for sure. People don't fit into neat little categories described in books. People are simply too complicated for that. People are not formulas, and the idea of labeling someone is ridiculous.

I felt my anger increasing but I caught myself and did

some deep breathing. In a few moments I was calmer. Tomorrow, when tomorrow comes I will get some answers. I repeated that over and over again until I convinced myself and felt better about things. I let it go and cleared my mind.

WHEN TOMORROW CAME I didn't get any answers because Dr. Allyson was called away on an emergency. I didn't get upset about not being able to see him I just accepted it. There was no energy left with which to get upset. It had all been spent the day before.

It was Wednesday and the student social worker came in on Wednesdays. Her name was Sandy. Sandy was tall and slender and wore straight skirts below the knee that made her appear even taller than she was. She had long wavy black hair which she wore pulled back behind a headband, big brown eyes filled with compassion, and rosy cheeks and lips that looked too red against pale skin. I took an instant liking to her the very first time we met. She told me a little bit about herself. She was working on her Master's degree. She was going to be a psychiatric social worker. She liked to ski.

Talking to Sandy was easy. I felt safe and comfortable with her. It was clear that she had a genuine concern for people, which is something one does not always encounter when one is in need of help. Sandy and I talked about different things but there was one question she asked me that really made me stop and think. She asked me if I would be able to recognize the onset of my illness if it should recur, would I be able to see it coming? I thought a long time about that and although I could not answer her then, because I didn't have any understanding of what had been happening to me, that very thing—understanding as much as I could—became the first priority of my life.

Days passed by uneventfully. Occasionally one of the inmates became agitated and a code was called and there would be a little excitement for an hour or two. The therapy aides played their guitars for us, and we sang songs sometimes on Saturday or Sunday. Not much happens when you live in a psychiatric hospital.

The worst part about being hospitalized was I had no goal. All of my needs were taken care of. I didn't have to do anything for myself except shower and eat and take medication. And I had to make my bed. After three months I was becoming institutionalized and the longer I was there the harder it would be when I got out. Thoughts of getting out of there became scary to me, the hospital had become my home in a way and what was really bad then was the powerful effect of the large doses of medication I was taking. It is impossible to convey in words the debilitating effects of these medications to anyone who has never had to take them. After those months of hospitalization and medication therapy I had lost the small motor coordination in my fingers. A simple task like tying a shoelace was impossible. The right side of my face would develop muscle spasms so that at times I looked like a freak, as my face became twisted and distorted. The medication affected the entire central nervous system. The process of elimination became compromised (certainly causing tremendous toxicity and a host of problems by itself). The hormonal balance was interrupted. The menses ceased. Symptoms of tardive-dyskinesis were developing (a serious condition leading to severe damage to the central nervous system including: Parkinson-like symptoms, rigidity of major muscles, loss of mental capacity with dulling of the senses and impaired memory function). In three months my life had become severely restricted. Now, however, it was time to go home and pick up the pieces. It was time for humpty dumpty to get back together again. It was time to be discharged.

"SO PATRICIA, TELL ME, what does 'a stitch in time saves nine' mean?"

I was sitting in the familiar brown leather chair staring at the wall behind Allyson's head. There was a new certificate hanging there. Now there were eight pieces of paper framed in black wooden squares, instead of seven.

Dr. Allyson wrote in my chart with quick sharp strokes to show the words he was writing who was boss. He wrote like a doctor. No one could read it. I knew that for sure, because I overheard Nurse Nancy one day complaining about his writing and how was she supposed to make certain the patients didn't drop dead from the wrong medication, especially when he never answered his phone messages.

I fidgeted a moment in the chair, searching around inside the empty cavern of my mind that had been hollowed out from Thorazine molecules and empty days of nothingness.

I couldn't make any connection between the words—stitch, time, nine.

I looked out the window. Oh for God's sake! Is it still winter? I took in a breath and held it for a few seconds. I thought about holding it until my face turned red and I passed out just so I could see Dr. Allyson's reaction. I exhaled instead—an idea popped into my mind. "Take care of things while they're still manageable, don't wait until they're out of control," I said.

Dr. Allyson kept pushing the black Parker across the paper, but now he penned his words in slow and easy strokes like he had made friends with them.

"OK Patricia, (he didn't look up but kept pushing) I'm going to let you go home on Friday. Sandy will make the arrangements for your discharge and aftercare."

Finally! Three months in this place and now freedom! I looked out the window again. Electric sunlight shimmered across the landscape, playing off ice crystals hanging from so many naked branches of oaks, hundreds of oaks, thousands of oaks, maybe a million oaks that stood there like still silent sentinels, frozen collectively into their annual death. Everywhere everything was dead, but the wind was alive and howling through the trees, making a fuss and a promise to maintain the ice crystals until the January thaw

88

claimed them for its own.

It seemed appropriate to me to be getting out of that place in the dead of winter. It was kind of symbolic after all. My life was like the landscape, dormant and frozen. But Spring was around the corner and the promise of a new beginning was waiting for me when I got out. I remembered Kandi's advice about asking questions, about not being afraid to ask the doctor what I needed to know. I wanted to know about medication and how long I would have to take that terrible stuff. I mustered up my courage. "How long will I need to remain on medication, Dr. Allyson?" I asked.

He didn't look up. I noticed he was starting to boss his words around again. "It will be best for you Patricia," he said, "if you remain on medication. You will have better stability that way. I've made arrangements for you to receive monthly injections of Prolixin as part of your aftercare program. Sandy will explain all of that to you."

Remain on medication! He wasn't serious was he? Why did I have to remain on medication? I never needed medication before! I couldn't even tie a shoelace because of medication! I was coaxing Quasimodo, and learning how to do it right. I could play the gal with Bell's palsy cause I could screw up my face real well without trying. I could shake and twitch and walk like the hunchback all right!

I could join the freak show at the circus. I'd be a cinch to get the job. Thank you very much—but no thanks!

I was furious again! What gave these doctors the right to play God with other people's lives? Who did they think they were anyway? I wanted to tell Dr. Allyson that he should try sitting on my side of his psychiatrist's desk, coaxing Quasimodo on 1200 milligrams of Thorazine a day. There had to be another way. There had to be another way and I would find it!

I knew Allyson was trying to help me, but I couldn't see it then. I looked at him in his white lab coat. Maybe he's not a real human being, I thought. Maybe he's a robot that only looks human. There was a name for those things but I couldn't think of it.

"Well, Patricia, I wish you good luck." Allyson looked up from his pushing, "And stay away from that religion!" Steel grey eyes that didn't blink but looked like cold fish stared at me with hollow intent. I looked back at him. The robot idea seemed to fit him pretty well. Oh yeah—he was an android all right! And without saying anything I got up from the brown leather chair for the last time and left his office.

Now what did he mean? What does religion have to do with anything? What is it that psychiatrists have against

God, I wondered? None of them believed in God. When you even mention the word God to a psychiatrist they automatically shrink down into their chairs as if they could prevent the word from getting close to them. You have to watch real carefully to see them do that because they don't want anyone to know they're afraid of anything, especially that. But I saw Allyson do it whenever I mentioned the word God. A line from Hamlet popped into my head. "There are more things in heaven and earth, Horatio, than are dreamt of in your philosophy."

As I left Allyson's office I promised myself I would find my own way and I would not be intimidated by the system. Receiving monthly injections of something called Prolixin was out of the question. I simply wouldn't do it.

KANDI WAS ON HER bed reading a letter from her husband. She looked up when she saw me come into the room. "Saw your doctor huh?" She said.

"Yeah, I'm going home on Friday."

She looked lovingly at the letter in her hand, folded it carefully in half and put it under her pillow. "So Pat," she said, "what are you going to do when you get out of this place?"

Take a slow boat to Japan, I thought to myself.

"I don't know, try and put my life back on track. But you know Kandi, this medication Dr. Allyson put me on makes me feel like a zombie. I can't hold a pen in my hand or sign my name, let alone write anything. I can't tie a shoelace, or zip a zipper. Sometimes I get muscle spasms in my face and I look like a freak! How am I supposed to live like this?"

"Did you tell the nurse?"

"Yeah, I'm getting medication for side effects, but it doesn't help!"

Kandi fixed her gaze on the ceiling above her head.

"Maybe there's a different drug you can take," she said. She began rolling her head in circles on her pillow. "Why don't you ask your doctor to try something else?"

"I did. He ordered a new drug for me when I go home, but if things don't get better, then the hell with the drugs."

Kandi pushed at her pillow trying to improve its disposition. "Be careful," she said. "You don't want to wind up back here again."

"Now you sound like them!" I was starting to get annoyed. I pulled a heavy sweater from my locker and put it on. I reached for my hooded jacket. It was purple with pink and black over-stitching on the seams. It was made from goose down and it was the warmest piece of clothing I owned. One of the patients had offered me a carton of cigarettes for it, and her dessert for a whole week.

"I'm taking a walk. See ya later, Kandi," I said.

"Brave girl! Don't freeze to death." She reached under her pillow and pulled out the letter from her husband. She read it every day even though he had not come to visit her the whole time she had been in the hospital.

OUTSIDE THE AIR WAS damp and heavy with coldness. Pregnant clouds darkened the January afternoon. It felt like snow. Sea gulls flew overhead. I felt sorry for them. They seemed so far away from home in the dead of winter, away from the shore. They belonged to the summertime, and looked like alien creatures lost in a season that didn't want them.

I pulled the hood of my jacket around my head snug and tight. The wind whipped at my clothes, teasing me, in frivolous amusement. My muscles tensed automatically from the cold, making me aware again of the compromised symmetry of the body shell I inhabited. I felt off balance.

I decided to ignore the wind and focused my attention on my footsteps: one, two, three, four—one, two, three, four—one, two, three, four.

My feet set the rhythm for my breath as I coordinated one with the other—inhale, one, two, three, four—exhale, one,

two, three, four—inhale, one, two, three, four. I lost awareness of the cold as I walked. My mind remained focused on
breath and rhythm. It felt good to be in control like that for
a few moments. There was no anger or fear or thought about
tomorrow. There was only body and breath and an awareness of how one became the other, of the rhythm of accord
between these two. The restless monkey mind that acted like
a naughty child and caused me so much trouble was under
my control and it felt good.

I headed towards the commissary. The endless stream of
people coming and going from that place was no longer
there, most of the patients remained inside. I continued to
walk-think. I continued to monitor monkey mind and breath.
Inhale, one, two, three, four—exhale, one, two, three, four.
Thoughts turned to review the last five years of my life, and
the events that landed me in Pilgrim. What could have
caused this strange change in my personality? Why had I
suddenly experienced a tremendous increase in energy that
made it impossible for me to sleep for three weeks? Could
it have been from taking LSD four times, four years earlier?
That idea seemed ridiculous. And how could I make sure I
never came back to Pilgrim? Hard to do that if one didn't
have a clue as to what brought one there to begin with. And
I certainly didn't have a clue.

I thought of Dr. Allyson—Alien Allyson. I wondered what psychiatrists learned about in school, besides medicine I mean. They didn't seem to understand people too well, and they certainly weren't friendly and they didn't smile very much either. And besides, what could anyone say about a person who bossed his words around across a piece of paper like that?

I resumed my rhythmic breathing. Inhale, one, two, three, four—exhale, one, two, three, four. Fifteen minutes passed. I turned back towards building 22 and that was when I realized suddenly, something had happened to the light. The grounds no longer had that magical look about them. There was a dull quality to the appearance of it all, so unlike the way things looked back in October.

It was more than the fact that the sunlight was diminished by the greying sky. It had been a long time since I had been able to perceive that wonderful light. Now It was just light—ordinary light—everyday—ordinary—mundane light that couldn't trip me into euphoria. I felt deprived. I missed that wonderful vision, that incredible high that came from some place, who knows where it came from?—but I wished it would come back to me.

I looked around one last time trying to recapture that wonderful experience of euphoria, but it was gone. If I only knew where that came from, boy, would I be doing something then! But I was a long way off from beginning to understand what had been happening to me. I had a long time to wait for answers to come.

PEOPLE WERE SINGING as I entered the day room. Pete and Sharon sat on the floor with their legs crossed injun style, strumming away on guitars while their bodies moved to the rhythm of string and sound. Some of the patients sat there with them, clapping their hands, some sat on the couches, some just stood around not sure what to do.

Sharon and Pete had gotten them all together but how they had done that I couldn't imagine. It was next to impossible to get people to participate in any group activity. But it was the music. Music had a special way of reaching people.

I joined the group. The song was a favorite of mine and one didn't get to sing in a group too often, when the fear of being heard off key was minimized by the sound of everyone else singing off key. Even Gloria was sitting in the corner listening, which was a big deal for Gloria.

Pete and Sharon continued playing for a while. I noticed some of the patients had fallen asleep lying there on the hard floor. Some had lost interest in the music and had turned their attention instead to the peculiarities and irregularities of the threadbare carpet underneath their bottoms. They liked to pick and pull at the loose fibers, rearranging the pattern as they went, especially enjoying their efforts when lengths of jute-like material could be pulled away from the backing.

Napoleon got up from his place on the couch and turned on the television, twisting the volume knob up all the way, which freaked Debbie out and she ran over to the electrical outlet and yanked the plug to the television right out of the wall. That got Napoleon agitated, so he took off his shoe and threw it at her nearly hitting her in the head. Then he made an awful face at her and stormed out of the room.

Nurse Nancy came along with her medication cart. She stood in the center of the room and yelled at the top of her lungs, "Med-i-caaaa-tion-every-one!"

It sounded like some one had stepped on her foot, and I swear she had a voice that could carry itself to China on a good day. That was the end of things for the moment and the impromptu concert was over.

Joyce Kramer had straight black hair pulled back behind her head into a pony tail that fell past her shoulders. She was trim and slender and wore turtlenecks tucked neatly into tight fitting jeans. I guessed her age to be about forty, but she looked like she was in her twenties.

Joyce Kramer's life was motivated by a sincere desire to help others, and it was my good fortune to have met her in January of 1974 when she was in the process of setting up a pilot program to help people who had been in places like Pilgrim State. I didn't know that the very first time I spoke with Joyce she was secretly interviewing me for the program.

I recall a short exchange of words between us and then her parting comment to me, "You're very lucky." I didn't know why Joyce thought I was lucky then, but if someone wanted to call me lucky I wasn't going to argue.

I was sitting in Sandy's office. It was on the north side of building 22 and freezing cold because the January wind blew straight across the open landscape of those trees with the ice crystals and right through cracks and gaps in the windows and vents. There was no insulation. The heating system was ancient and inadequate.

Sandy sat in front of me, looking like a stuffed sausage in her heavy woolen sweater zippered up to her chin.

"Well Pat," she began, "you have an opportunity to attend a pilot program with five other people in Cedarhurst. It's a program that begins at nine in the morning and ends at three thirty in the afternoon, Monday through Friday. It will be run by Joyce. I believe she has had the opportunity to meet with you?"

"Yes, I met with her yesterday." I fidgeted in the cold metal folding chair.

"If you're accepted into this program and you do well you may have an opportunity to go to school. There's a link program Joyce is working on through the Office of Vocational Rehabilitation which will help the clients of her program get into school after they have finished. It's an excellent opportunity for you, Pat. Do you think you'd like to try it?"

I thought about going to school—college. Now that was something I was interested in, not like dull and boring high school, student stabbings, and armed security guards in the halls.

"It sounds like a wonderful idea to me," I said.

"OK Pat. I'll start on the paper work this afternoon."

As I stood up to leave, Sandy came out from behind her desk and shook my hand. "Good luck to you Pat," she said. "Drop me a note and let me know how you're doing."

I thought about being lucky just then. I realized that if I was lucky, it was because of all the great people I met along the way in my life.

I WAS SITTING in the day room. Two more days—two more for me and I'm outta here! I looked around the room and saw Napoleon sleeping on a chair at the far end. Gloria was sitting on the floor in the corner rocking back and forth to her own internal rhythm. She had dumped an ash tray out on the floor all around her looking for a butt. She was sitting in the mess.

Paula, the woman with the abandonment issue, was out on a pass and wouldn't be back until the next day. The depressed man was no longer with us. He had gone home for the holidays and had never come back. He hanged himself at home on New Year's Eve. Marion, the lady that lost her husband, had been discharged. She went to live with her sister even though she didn't want to because there was no place else for her to go. Debbie was still there. She didn't believe she was the Virgin any more. Now she believed she was from a different planet and she couldn't eat any food because it would poison her, but for some strange reason she would eat graham crackers. As I got up to leave the room I said a silent farewell to the inmates of building 22.

I WAS ON THE COUCH in the visitors' lounge. Old Soul came in, sat down next to me, and threw a deck of cards on the table in front of us.

"Hey Pat, I heard you're finally getting out of this place on Friday."

"Oh yeah, and who told you anyway?"

"I know everything that goes on here," he said fumbling with the cellophane wrapping on the cards.

"So tell me, David, what about you? What are you going to do? What are your plans?"

He pulled two jokers from the deck and began shuffling. "I'm supposed to go to a halfway house in Brooklyn. I don't really want to go to the city, but I'll deal with it."

I fished around inside my pocket and pulled out a pack of cigarettes. "You know, David, if it wasn't for you being here I think I really would be crazy. You were the only person I could talk to, you and Kandi. Life is real simple in a place like this. What really matters is easy to see here. It's not what's out there, it's not what's out there in the world of things, it's what's inside, inside one's own heart—what we can give to one another—what we can share with each other. And when we can't share with one another, when we don't communicate, when we speak a language different from the rest, then we're lost. Life is about relationships, about sharing what we have, whatever it is, and realizing whatever it is we have, it's perfect just the way it is. And you know, David, I have really become aware of how important communication skills are. I never thought about it before, but people need to be taught how to communicate. It's not just learning how to speak, is it? People can speak words without communicating. I saw that in group. Napoleon spoke to John but communicated very little except raw anger."

David put his feet up on the table, and folded his arms across his chest. "If someone can't communicate, they probably can't get their needs met, which will eventually lead to frustration and anger. And that goes on all the time here, doesn't it?"

"I guess it goes on all the time everywhere," I said, pulling a cigarette from my pack and offering one to him.

"Thanks." He smiled his words at me. "How about a game of Rummy?"

We played cards until supper time. No one interrupted us. No one tried to get in on the game. Every once and a while Pete would walk by and look in. Things were calm and quiet, until after dinner.

IT WAS EIGHT O'CLOCK. Napoleon had been restless since before we went to the dining hall. It started around the time the nurse called for meds. As soon as she called Napoleon over to her he became agitated, he didn't want to take his medication again. And even though she managed to get him to take it without too much trouble, everyone could see he was upset.

The nurse decided to keep Napoleon on the unit during dinner that night, she didn't want to take a chance with him getting more upset in the dining hall. But Napoleon didn't understand that part of it and he just got angrier.

Later on when we all got back from supper Napoleon was strapped into a geri chair. It's called a geri chair because it's used a lot with older patients who need to keep their feet elevated and because they can be restrained by a food tray wedged up against their middles, which works really well for disoriented people who need to be kept safe.

But Napoleon wasn't disoriented, he was angry. His feet were tied down and his hands were wedged underneath the meal tray. He had thrown his plate full of food at Pete when it was handed to him. So now he was strapped and wedged tight. The plate lay upside down on the floor three feet from the chair. Pot roast with mashed potatoes and gravy, peas and carrots and vanilla ice cream made a food collage across the shiny waxed tiles.

"Bastards, bastards! They're all bastards! They're commies and they're gonna eat dirt! Bastards eat dirt! Oh shut up stupid! I don't wanna talk to you, commie bastard!" Napoleon looked at Pete as he yelled and fought against the tray that pinned his arms. As he struggled to free his hands from beneath the tray, cuts in the flesh of his forearms began to appear. He was bleeding. Pete went over to him to try and calm him down, but that was useless. Napoleon became even more agitated.

Inside the fishbowl the nurse was preparing a needle. It was what was called an injection PRN. That meant that whenever anyone misbehaved they could be medicated at the nurse's discretion. The nurse's discretion said it was time for Napoleon's PRN.

It just so happened that on that particular day, the evening shift in building 22 was short staffed. There were only two people available to assist the nurse as she attempted to give Napoleon an injection in his arm.

It is remarkable how strong a person can be when he is agitated like Napoleon was that night. He decided that he was not going to be medicated and fought with all his strength against the determined effort of those three people. In his struggle Napoleon managed to tip his chair over backwards onto the floor, something that was not too hard to do when it was in the reclining position. In the excitement Pete had forgotten to return the chair to its upright position. Pete fell on top of Napoleon when the chair fell over, and

Napoleon let out the most awful inhuman screeching sound I ever heard. And you can just guess what had to happen next, with Pete's head being in such close proximity to Napoleon's mouth. Well, Napoleon managed to get hold of Pete's ear with his teeth and Napoleon was not gentle. Pete let out a scream that was even more terrible sounding than the one that came from Napoleon. It was almost impossible to see who was who, with arms, hands and legs flying around here and there. And all the while the other aide frantically attempted to free Pete's ear from Napoleon's terrible grip.

Meanwhile the nurse was fussing about with the needle and hesitating for too long, I'm sure, because of her fear of putting that needle where it didn't belong. But finally she managed to bury it in Napoleon's arm. That distracted Napoleon just enough so that the aide could finally help Pete save his ear from that awful mouth.

The whole thing ended as quickly as it began leaving Napoleon with the wind knocked out of him from the fall. Pete required medical attention for the prevention of infection from a human bite. And the nurse, well, she was good and angry at the lack of staff and the fact that the incident had to be reported, making her evening even more hectic than it was already.

Napoleon was allowed to remain on the floor next to his spilled dinner until he was unconscious. It took five minutes for the injection to work, and then he was taken to the dormitory. The spilled dinner was cleaned up and the excitement for the evening was over.

Thirty-six hours later I was sitting with David saying my goodbye's. Mother would be arriving any minute, and I would be gone from Pilgrim. I would miss him.

"You know, David, when I first came to this place, well I was so confused, there was so much going on in my mind. I had this tremendous psychic energy that wouldn't quit. It was as if my mind was overloaded with information and couldn't file it properly so nothing was making any sense. At the same time, though, there was this kind of euphoria that was enhanced when I went outside into the sunlight. It was the most extraordinary experience I have ever had. It was like being in heaven. It's all gone, all of it. The confusion is gone but so is the euphoria. How is it I could feel so wonderful and confused at the same time?"

"You're talking about kundalini energy."

I had heard that word before, Jana had used it. "A friend of mine mentioned that once. What is that David?"

There was a long pause. David seemed to be searching for the proper words. "It's a kind of psychic energy that has been described for thousands of years. It's a Hindu idea. They believe there exists a reservior of untapped energy available to the personality, but it's often unused by the average individual. It's an energy of creativity, the driving force for the process of individuation of the personality—a way to attain a spiritual state if you will. But it takes training and discipline to be able to properly utilize this energy. It's a very serious matter. The closest concept we have in the West is Freud's libido, but our society is far away from understanding these ideas. We are relatively underdeveloped in the West when it comes to a deeper wisdom."

I thought about the energy idea for a minute and it did make sense to me. "So you mean this confusion and this euphoria is something called kundalini?"

Gloria walked into the room looked at us then turned around and walked out.

"The euphoria was, but the confusion, well, that's what you have to work on."

I studied his handsome profile for a moment. "But what does all of this have to do with sex?" I asked.

He corrected me. "I said libido, not sex. Libido is a biological energy which is the same energy as kundalini. Energy is energy. It only changes as it expresses itself through different organs. For example, when energy is expressed through the heart we call it love."

I felt like my brain was on overload again. Whenever I talked with David I could always count on that reaction.

"I think this is all very fascinating David, and it's really quite deep. I'll have to learn about it a little at a time, but it makes sense to me."

"You know what's so ironic about all of this?"

I was afraid he was going to tell me. "I can't begin to guess David. What?"

"What's ironic, is that the people in this place have tremendous potential for development of kundalini energy, but not one of them knows anything about it. Their illnesses are a manifestation of that energy, but it's out of control. They are gifted people, but they don't know how to use the gift they have—the creative energy they possess—so it turns on them and takes them over. That's what is so ironic."

I wondered how it might ever be possible to view the affliction of mental illness as a gift. That was where I drew the line. That made no sense to me.

"It's really a lot to think about David. I'll have to reserve my judgement."

"One day you'll know what I'm talking about, Pat."

He just kept smiling at me. I smiled back at him, asking

myself as I had done many times over the past three months, who is he?

"Hey, Old Soul," I said, "keep in touch will you?"

"When I get settled in Brooklyn I'll call you. My counselor promised me I'll be out of here by the end of this month."

I looked at David's face into those pale green eyes. They were calm and gentle and held a deeper wisdom than I could imagine. We gave one another a hug. I went to the dormitory to finish packing, knowing I would never see him again.

"ARE YOU SURE YOU have everything, sweetie?"

God, I loved my mother but I wished she would stop calling me sweetie. I was too old to be a sweetie. But it was a control thing with Mother. She couldn't help it.

Mother opened and closed the drawers of my night stand. Kandi came into the dormitory and flung herself down on the bed. "Remember Pat," she said, "don't be afraid to ask, ask, ask, anything you need to know. It's the only way to salvation. Pick their brains for everything you can get."

"Mom, you remember Kandi?"

Mother smiled at her and continued looking around the room for anything I might have forgotten.

Kandi reached under her pillow and pulled out a small

object. It was a tiny owl carved from ivory. "It's for good luck on your quest for understanding," she said, handing it to me.

I looked closely at it and saw mysterious dark red eyes with gold rings in the centers. Some of the markings from the artist's blade seemed to resemble tiny letters. I couldn't make them out. I put the owl in my pocket. I looked at my friend sitting there and I knew somehow just then, that things would work out for her. I went over and hugged her goodbye for the last time.

Pete's keys clanked against the dead bolt in the double doors that led to the long straight corridor of freedom from building 22.

"No offense Pat, but I hope I never see you again." Pete offered me his hand.

"Yeah, me too," I said, accepting his goodbye gesture.

He turned towards Mother. "Good bye Mrs. Bloise," he said.

"Good bye Pete," Mother replied, and smiled a simple goodbye as she walked away.

WE WERE DRIVING WEST on the Sagtikos parkway. The world was frozen. The landscape looked like a giant skating rink, and as I watched the scenery unfolding around me at sixty miles an hour I realized nothing had changed. The parkway looked the same. All the road signs looked the same. No new towns had sprung up in the three months of my confinement.

Isn't it funny how the things we come back to almost want to tell us it's just your imagination, you've been here the whole time, you just think you've been gone for a while. Change marks time for us. We are creatures of change, that's what tells us we're alive. Like when something really big happens—like if a giant sinkhole swallows a small city or something and it's here one day, gone the next, then you really get a sense of progression. I mean when old things go then there's room for the new. My life was letting go of something pretty big and now it was time to make room for the new. I had my freedom back.

Or did I?

It occurred to me while Mother drove the car at sixty miles an hour on the Sagtikos parkway, that I would never be free as long as I was a slave to my thoughts; as long as I was unable to control my mind, that monkey mind that ran me ragged and spun my wheels into Wonderland, I would be a prisoner, a prisoner inside my own head. Old fish-face Allyson's answer was easy: he just wanted me to be reigning queen of zombie land. But guess what Allyson—keep your crown. The side effects of those medications were a disability I couldn't live with.

Still I was afraid. What if he was right? What if I stopped taking the drugs and lost it? What if I went back down the rabbit hole? None of this makes sense, none of it, none of it, none of it, damn it....

I WAS IN MY ROOM. My old room. On my old bed in Mother's house looking at that wall of mine. What a disorganized mess that wall is, I thought. Bright colors that were too strong offended my sensibilities. I was used to dull and boring hospital-yellow. The wall made me nervous. I was going to have to paint.

Reorienting—I was quietly reorienting—alone and by myself. Mother had taken my son David visiting friends and I was in my old room, in a state of utter and complete disgust. Here I was at nineteen years of age and my life was a disaster. What a mess I had made of things—a mess, a mess, a mess. The best part of the situation was, I realized then, there was only one way to go.... only one way to go but...

THE B15 BUS FROM Long Beach to Cedarhurst was three minutes late and I was freezing to death. It was ten degrees but the wind chill was minus eighteen. Three minutes is an eternity at eighteen below, especially when you forget your scarf.

I stood there like a frozen popsicle, the wind wrapped itself around my body, biting the skin of my face. My eyes were burning. Tears ran down my cheeks. I tried to make the bus materialize by the power of my will, but it didn't work.

I pulled a cigarette from my pocket and managed to light it in spite of my thick gloves. Just then the B15 turned the corner and headed my way.

Alice, Tammy, Peter, Jeff and Michael were already in the house when I got there. They were sitting around the kitchen table sipping coffee while Joyce spoke to them about the scheduled activities for the week coming up—the first week of our new program—the program Joyce had developed to help people adjust to normal living (normal living?) after periods of confinement in a psychiatric hospital. I sat at the table with the others and listened to Joyce explain her hopes for us, what was expected of us, and our responsibilities while we were together. She was an inspiration. She became our mentor, our counselor, our friend.

As time passed friendships formed between us. We talked together about our problems, cooked our meals,

washed dishes, kept journals, set goals that were unobtain-
able, set goals that were realistic, cried about our problems,
felt sorry for ourselves, vented our feelings, developed an
understanding of each other, about the commonality of our
problems, and found strength there.

It was a time of healing—from too much sensitivity. Too
much sensitivity can kill you. But it can also be your
greatest ally if you learn how to use it, guard it, honor it.
That's what Joyce wanted to teach us. About our potential,
which we couldn't appreciate because it got turned around
the wrong way in a world that admires the worst in us,
instead of the best—in a society gone mad. Survival for
sensitives depends on a strong defense against the dis-ease
of society. There is a way to do that—it's the Way of Love.
Something that was discovered by a genius of a man who
lived and walked this earth two thousand years ago. That's
what each of us needed to learn. How to love ourselves.

I MET LETTI ON THE B15 bus from Cedarhurst to Long
Beach one late afternoon in March. It was a Friday, I think,
and the B15 was filled with city commuters on their way to
the weekend. Letti moved over in her seat when she saw me
walking down the aisle and I took it as an invitation to sit
down. She was friendly in an easy sort of way, for a

stranger. Her clothes were brightly colored. Orange and
yellow silks that were fine and delicate wrapped her plump
womanhood in modesty. She was that—modest and naive
and so un-American. Her eyes were big, black and
sparkley—unassuming I thought—and promised to have
fun with the world in a playful sort of way. I could see her
girlish soul in them, the soul of a child. Letti spoke with an
accent, it sounded Asian, kind of thick and beautiful and it
brought images to my mind of shapely belly dancers and
thin dark men with sun-bleached cotton turbans on their
heads.

We sat together that first day and talked as if we had
known each other forever. There was a strange kind of
familiarity between us, even though she was from Koraput
on the east coast of India and I knew absolutely nothing
about where she came from and could not begin to imagine
what kind of life a young woman might have there.

Letti admitted she liked living in the United States,
because she didn't have to get up before dawn to care for
her Auntie Loma, which had been a hardship to her for
many years when she was living in India. And she didn't
have to pray for rain that never fell from empty skies,
whose one gift to the scorching earth below was to swallow
the sun every night only to spit it back out again the next

day. She told me that it was a very unusual bit of good fortune that had allowed her to come to the United States. People from her place in life, she said, lived and died in their poverty never moving beyond the parameters of their own lack, never moving beyond their own acceptance of what life held for them. Now in America she lived like a Brahmin, enjoying the luxury of running water and electricity. She had her own room for sleeping and a table to sit at for meals.

Letti said she prayed to Kali every day to take away old things and bring new ones. She wanted a new life in her new country, but she thought it was a terrible pity that such a big country with so many people had become so mixed up and had no worship that seemed to do any good. Where were the Gurus, the teachers? What had happened to the spirit of the people in the West she wanted to know.

I tried to explain to her while I sat there, that I had wondered about that very thing myself and I was sorry I was not better informed.

Letti stopped talking as the bus came to a halt. I looked out the window and was surprised to see it was time for me to get off. She looked at me apologetically and spoke almost in a whisper: "But now I have talked too much to you stranger. Forgive my rudeness, please. I am so sorry."

When she got up from her seat next to me I realized she was getting off the bus too. She lived in Long Beach and we were neighbors. I liked that idea.

"HOW ABOUT A CUP of tea, sweetie?"

Mother was sitting at the kitchen table dragging a pencil eraser over a *New York Times* crossword puzzle. It was left over from the week before, but Mother never gave up on those things until they were done.

I pulled two bags of Earl Grey from the cupboard, two cups from the clean side of the dishwasher, and put the tea kettle on.

Mother sat there scribbling in the little boxes. "What's a five-letter word for rattling chains after midnight?" She said staring at the empty little squares.

I rolled my eyeballs into the top of my head hoping to find the correct letters hiding out there. "How about G-H-O-S-T?" I offered.

"Ah ha!" she exclaimed, happy like a little kid. She looked up from her puzzle. "What time do you have to see the nurse tomorrow, Pat?" she asked.

I sucked in a breath—hard. Angry words flew from my mind almost coming out of my mouth but I caught myself. Damn it Mother, do you have to remind me! I didn't want to talk about it, I didn't want her to notice that I had given in and decided to keep the appointment Dr. Allyson made for me in the local clinic. I wished she wouldn't ask, wouldn't say it. Why didn't she just keep quiet about it anyway? My mood soured. The tea kettle started to whistle. I went to my room.

It didn't bother me that I was sitting in my room by myself. So what if it was eight o'clock on a Saturday night? I didn't mind because I actually enjoyed being alone in my own company. I usually had little trouble entertaining myself. But I was not happy that night. I was disappointed in myself for giving in. What was I going to do? I had no choice. I didn't have enough information about what happened to me to decide if it was safe to stop the medication. I just didn't know enough.

THE NURSE SAID HER name was Mrs. Hardmond. She was wearing a green turtleneck sweater underneath a matching green jacket, and a green skirt. Her jet black hair was done up in a French knot with shiny stick pins and a ton of hair spray. She looked like a kiwi.

Nurse Hardmond smiled a big nursey smile, the kind the friendly ones can manage, whipped out her needle and before I could say left or right decided with eagle eye precision which centimeter of skin would receive her blessing. She was not as practiced as Nurse Nancy, of building 22.

"Ouch!" I yelled, trying not to be rude.

"You have to remember to relax, honey."

She sounded like my mother.

"See you in a month, Patricia," she said as she disposed of the offending syringe.

I hope not, I thought as I left the clinic rubbing the spot on my behind that was surely already turning black and blue from Mrs. Hardmond's nursing.

I stared out the window of the bus all the way home. The passing images erased the thoughts from my mind, like some giant hand pulling taffy out from the center of my forehead. I didn't want to think. I didn't want to play this game called mental illness. I had to strengthen my position. I went to the library.

"Can you please reserve these books for me?" I handed Lady Librarian my list of twenty-five titles from the card catalogue. She was annoyed right away.

"You cannot expect me to reserve all these books for you!"

"Why not?" I asked in a mildly defiant tone of voice.

"Because patrons are only allowed five books out on loan

at one time," she snorted at me.

"Well then, I'll just take the five off the top."

Lady Librarian puckered her mouth, curling the ends of her pudgy red lips for added emphasis. She took the list away and after about five minutes came back with a slip. She handed me the piece of paper."We'll call you when they come in," she said, puckering her pudgy lips at me for a second time. Then she walked away.

I HAD NEVER SEEN hair the color of a tangerine before. And no freckles. How unusual, I thought.

I was being processed for rehabilitation. The lady with the tangerine hair said her name was Meena Thompson, she was a Case Worker III, this was the office of Vocational Rehabilitation and, no, I was not allowed to smoke in her office. Her job was to process forms—and the people who came into her office with the forms. My job was to pay attention and listen so we could finish and she could go to lunch.

I was having trouble paying attention. Quasimodo was trying to visit with me while I sat there. I was having a muscle spasm in my face. I kept it pointed at the floor waiting for it to be normal again. I didn't want to frighten the case worker even though I was sure she had seen plenty of funny things in her day. This interview was important. I was trying to make a good impression. I was to be rehabilitated.

It didn't make me feel too special to think that I was someone who had to be rehabilitated, like a criminal or something. Case Worker III could have found a better way to describe her processing of me. But then I was not in a position to argue. After all, my future was at stake here. I wanted to go to school.

Case Worker III swiveled in her seat with the grace of a penguin, bent down to the file cabinet beside her knee, jerked open the drawer, pulled out a green folder and waved it in the air.

"See? Empty! When is Joyce Kramer going to send her report on you?"

I kept my face pointed at the floor. "Gee, Mrs. Thompson, I don't know."

"It's Miss, not Mrs. and what's the matter with you? Why are you staring like that?"

"I have a stiff neck, excuse me. I'm sure Joyce has sent you all the papers for processing by now."

"Well that isn't so. Please tell her to call me this week so I can finish up and get done with you. Now fill this out and write neatly. Here's a pen."

I began in earnest to complete my assignment. It was

hard to write because my hand was stiff from my medication.

"You're very lucky, you know." Case Worker III was staring at me. "There was only one slot left for this program and the administrator of this section doesn't even like Joyce Kramer. I don't know how you got in."

I blinked my eyes at her wondering if she had secretly disposed of the form Joyce sent so I couldn't get into my slot.

"Are you finished yet, dear?"

She called me dear. I hated to be called that. Did I have antlers growing out from my scalp now? I completed the form and signed my name on the back. It looked like the signature of a six-year-old. I handed it to Case Worker III. She put the form in the empty folder, slipped it into the file cabinet and closed the drawer. I heard her stomach growling and it sounded like she hadn't eaten in a week.

Case Worker III got up from her chair. "We're done for now, sweetie," she said.

As I left the office I couldn't help but wonder when Meena Thompson had spoken with my mother.

I STARED OUT THE window of the B35 all the way home and thought about going to school. God, could I really and do well? My brain felt like it was in slow gear most of the time. How was I going to study and absorb? Reading for pleasure was one thing, but taking tests! Damn this medication! I looked at my hand. I opened and closed my fist. Stiff fingers tried to deny their composition of joints, tendons and muscles by remaining fixed and inflexible. I pushed at them. They obeyed me with resistance. A bony protrusion slid back and forth underneath pink skin unable to deny the marvel of evolutionary mechanics—an opposable thumb! How lucky I am to have this thumb, I thought. But big deal! I still can't hold a pen very well! How am I going to write with the speed of a student in her freshman year of college?

Damn you, Allyson! Couldn't you have told me something else? Couldn't you have explained how it was possible for me to have lived a normal life before I met you? Couldn't you have had the courage to step out beyond the safety of your own indoctrination, of your own personal, yes—religion! How was it that I was a normal ordinary nineteen-year-old struggling to pull her life together, someone who had made mistakes, OK, I admit it, but not hopeless ones and now after meeting you fish-face I'm a crazy nineteen-year-old whose life is in a shambles?

I made my decision right then on the bus—no more Prolixin.

I SKIPPED THE appointment for my shot. The earth didn't stand still. My brain didn't catch on fire. The mind police didn't descend on me. I kept my control. Life moved along.

I ran into Letti on the bus one day and we talked the whole time with that uncanny familiarity. She said we knew each other in a past life, that was why we felt so at home together. We started having brunch on Sundays.

I got my old job back at night, punching keys on the register at Julia Waldbaum's supermarket. The customers were easy at night. They didn't whine about ice cream bags —don't you have any, honey? Can you please lay that flat? Don't bump my apples or the bananas—don't put that there—never put Tidy Bowl with the bread—don't they train you here?

One day at home I stopped what I was doing right in the middle of it, I think it was dishes, and started to cry and say thank you to God for giving me my life back.

I know this sounds silly but I really mean it. I was grateful for just being OK. I was happy. I had achieved a small victory for myself. Quasimodo couldn't bother me anymore.

LETTI AND I WERE going to the movies to see a low budget trashy film made in Australia. I rang her doorbell and she answered saying, "Come in for tea, Pat, please. Ahead you are of the time."

The smell of incense made me feel at home right away. I took off my shoes by the door like she asked and sat on the floor of her living room cross-legged on top of a black silk pillow trimmed in gold. It had sixteen tassels, four on each side.

"That is a very special pillow," she said pointing at it. Letti told me the pillow represented the four elements: earth, water, fire and air, and that when she meditated on it she went to heaven. I wondered where I could get a pillow like that.

"How do you get to heaven on a pillow?" I wanted to know.

"It takes practice, and you have to sit a long time. There's a long line to get in." She brought us tea and cookies.

I went to the bathroom to wash my hands. I passed by her

room, and there on the wall facing me was a photograph of the most beautiful human being I had ever seen. My heart stopped for a moment.

"That is my Guru," Letti said standing behind me. Her face was glowing.

gu-ru\ge-'rü, gu(e)r-(.)ü\ *n, pl* **gurus** [Hindi *guru*, fr. Skt *guru*, fr. *guru*, adj., heavy, venerable — more at GRIEVE] 1: a personal religious teacher and spiritual guide in Hinduism... (By permission. From Merriam-Webster's Collegiate ® Dictionary, 10th Ed. ©1997 by Merriam-Webster, Incorporated.)

A Guru is not just a teacher, Letti explained to me one day. A Guru is someone who helps an individual achieve a personal relationship with God. She told me that it was very dangerous to try and find God by yourself, that you needed a guide, someone who can show the way, because the way is dangerous.

Everyone has a Guru she said and sooner or later each of us will find him. When we do we will know and then we will begin our true journey.

Letti was such a happy person I figured her Guru must have been helping her find God. Anyway, whatever Letti was doing with her Guru it seemed to be working. I hoped one day I could be happy like that.

Patricia Anne Bloise

I SPENT FOUR SEMESTERS at Nassau Community College on Long Island majoring in Early Childhood Education, where I learned a lot about how children grow up and become well adjusted and about the best ways to teach them the things they need to learn.

The most important thing I learned is that above all else a child needs love and structure. An orderly world makes for a sound mind.

Maria Montessori demonstrated that pretty well with her exceptional teaching methods that helped children excel in learning. But I already understood by then how important it is that the world makes sense to us, but especially to young children, who need to have a sense of order so they can grow properly.

I transferred to Hofstra University after my graduation from Nassau and decided I didn't want to teach elementary school after all. Somehow it wasn't for me. I wanted to study psychology. I mean, who was going to climb into my head and straighten out the mess and give me a sense of order?

It was lucky for me that the psychology department at Hofstra was run by two fabulous women who were definitely not behaviorists, but who leaned towards the more esoteric theorists, my favorites, Freud and his buddies.

I paid attention in school this time. I studied at home

every minute. Learning became a burning compulsion. I was on track again to be Miss Know It All. I hadn't learned my lesson the first time around. I was still at it, still trying to absorb a universe of information, still trying to find the pieces of my puzzle, to make sense of my senseless world.

FREUD WAS MAKING me depressed. I understood from all my learning that I could never have a good marriage because I never had a father. Because I never had a father, I never learned how to overcome penis envy, so I never conquered Oedipus. Well something like that.

Freud said some other things that made sense to me though. He said that the infant child possesses a kind of immature cosmic consciousness because the sense receptors in his brain aren't developed and that when the infant feels anything he feels it as his whole universe. The infant has no sense of "I" as a separate entity. His connection is to everything. He is the god of his universe. I guess Freud would say we're all just trying to remember what we had as infants.

I hated logic, but I loved anatomy and physiology. I hated philosophy, but I had a crush on the teacher. School was great the first year. The second year depression came.

My ex-husband David was in a fatal accident leaving me in a state of disbelief that God could remove him from my life. I still had very deep feelings for him and it was a tremendous loss to me. He was only twenty-five.

A terrible darkness descended on me. There are no words to describe my feelings then. I went to a shrink and told him all about my problems. He decided that Lithium would help me. It didn't.

My life became a source of pain again. My love of learning could not override my grief, I had no way to cope with my feelings. I couldn't make sense of the world, or of my place in it.

Sleeping became less restful and there was this awful nightmare I had about David being stuck in some terrible place without light. I cried and felt miserable for him because of my lack of understanding, because I couldn't explain what happened to him and didn't know then that there is a Grace that carries us above all our troubles and that God's love never fails His children.

I prayed in my Catholic way in rote fashion as I had been taught. I prayed from fear of the dark for him and for me. I prayed that the world would not come undone, that tomorrow I would wake up and the sun would still hold its bright place in the sky, that the planet earth would remain forever our living mother, whether or not we, her ungrateful children, were honorable in our hearts. I prayed for understanding.

I WAS HAVING BRUNCH with Letti. "You know Patti, you should learn how to meditate, it will make you feel better. Oh yes, and take a walk, there is nothing better for your health. Don't stick in your room full of books. Go in the sun and breathe the air deep into your lungs. Would you like more tea Patti?"

I loved Letti. She was the sister I never had. Her playful attitude and bright cheerfulness probably saved me from going deeper into my despair for a while.

I never told Letti about what happened to me in the hospital, about my craziness, about getting lost in time. I never told her about the things Old Soul talked about.

I tried to come to terms with David's death. I tried to mend my broken heart. But I was too weak then, too confused, too unsure of my place in the world.

I crossed the threshold of pain into numbness. No tears were left. No songs to sing. No joy. No hope. No light. The pain in my heart for my son's father ran deep and dragged me down into the darkness. I cycled up and down recovering some energy, but losing it again, only to spiral down farther than the time before. It took eighteen months of cycling in small orbits before the mania came again taking me down the rabbit hole.

IT IS PECULIAR THE sorts of things that can go on in the mind of a manic person. I always get clogged in the head. All my energy sort of gets stuck above the sixth vertebra in my neck. I figure it has something to do with that time I meditated and went into the tunnel, but I don't really know if that's the reason. But it makes sense that it had to do some kind of damage.

Well anyway, I don't remember how it began the second time, how much sleep I missed, what kind of crazy business I was dreaming up that time. I only remember waking up in the hospital with my mother sitting next to me.

There was an odd sense of restriction, the way one might feel without arms and hands, without symmetry or grace, like a five-pointed star reduced to only three points. My middle was wrapped and strapped tight.

"Hey ma, what is this?" I asked.

"You were trying to fly out of your body sweetie. I was afraid you were going to kill yourself the way you were running down the hall backwards trying to fly out of your body. I asked the nurse to do something about it."

I knew that wasn't the case at all. It was just that I had gotten stuck in the memory of my training in gymnastics. It was the time I was trying to learn the back flip that did it. How could I explain that to her?

"Tell them to come and get me out of this, please mother!"

She ignored me. "Did you enjoy your birthday party?"

"What birthday party?" I asked.

"You don't remember your birthday party? It's from the shock treatments—that's why you can't remember."

I was really starting to freak now. "Shock treatments?"

There was a long hesitation. "Yes, you had nine of them."

Thirty seconds passed, then the world went dark.

MY AUNT ALBA hated my doctor. One time when she had this little nervous condition and she was not feeling well, her son took her to see this doctor, the same one that wound up treating me in '79. Well, this doctor said she needed to have shock treatments, but she refused. Aunt Alba said he was a crazy man and just wanted to do that to everybody.

It was a funny coincidence the way we both got to be treated by the same crazy doctor. Me and Aunt Alba had some good laughs together about the whole thing. My aunt is a very funny lady.

I spent three weeks at Hempstead General Hospital, but I don't remember much of anything except that it was quiet there and the food wasn't bad. I was like a zombie then, between those drugs they put me back on and the additional "treatments."

I had managed to earn a relatively consistent diagnosis. The second time around it was Schizoaffective disorder, and I guess you might say there had been a little progress.

The crazy doctor wrote orders for my transfer to Hillside Hospital in Glen Oaks, the psychiatric facility for Long Island Jewish Medical Center in New Hyde Park, because it would have been impossible for me to go home in the condition I was in and Hempstead General's program was short term. The police took me to Hillside. I didn't mind. I felt safe with them.

I was admitted to an open unit—no locked doors. It was on the first floor of a small brick building. I remember very clearly the first night I was there. I was taking a shower and I was alone, no one was around. My mind was filled with confusion. An avalanche of ideas jumbled loose from some dark cavern of my consciousness. I felt a haunting presence. It was fear, obscure at first, but as it began to take shape and define itself, it swept me into a panic. Something was wrong in my mother's house. It was my son. Something was terribly wrong with my son. He was being cared for by his grandmother, I knew he was with her, but there was something else, some danger there with him. I couldn't sense clearly what it was, which magnified the fear in me.

My emotional self took control. The little bit of ego that was me went underground. I knew somehow, I had to get to Long Beach. I had to get home and make sure my son was OK.

I reached toward the wall, turned off the water and stood there for a moment dripping wet. There was no inner voice of reason, only the muted presence of instinct that spoke to me from deep within my primitive brain. It seemed as if someone else had taken control of my body, some other personality had taken over and I could do nothing but watch what was happening.

In a trance-like state, I walked out of the shower area, down the hallway to the double swing doors of the building and out into the night. I was displaced in space and time again. Although my consciousness was housed in the baggage of flesh and bone it did not identify itself with the vessel. My body was part of me, but not part of me, and the physical vehicle that I possessed was only an inconvenient restriction that kept me on the physical plane.

Fifty yards in front of me stood an eight-foot chain link fence. Like a cat in the night I was over it and on the other side of freedom.

I was walking down 76th Avenue stark naked, bare footed and my hair was dripping wet. I was going to Long Beach. How I was supposed to get there was irrelevant.

THE ANGELS WATCHED over me that night when a young man on his way to New Jersey stopped his car and picked me up. There was no fear in me, no thought that I might put myself in danger, there were only thoughts of my boy.

"I have to get to Long Beach," I told him desperately.

"Get in," he said opening the car door for me. He looked at me with wide non-believing eyes as I climbed into the front seat of his car. He didn't say anything to me for a time. He just drove.

I sat there quietly staring out the windshield at highway lights flashing by. There were no thoughts, no words in my mind. It had become like the ocean depths, still and dark.

Minutes passed and he finally spoke. "I'm a disc jockey," he said, "and if I told my listeners that I picked up a beautiful naked woman walking down 76th Avenue tonight they'd never believe me." He was glaring at me in a polite way.

He continued speaking to me, "I have to make a run to New Jersey and after that I'll take you to Long Beach." He kept staring at me with those non-believing eyes.

All went well until we approached a toll booth, and my rescue angel realized the seriousness of driving around in his car with a naked woman. He pulled over to the far side of the road, stopped for a moment, and reached behind the seat for a newspaper. I think it was the *New York Times*.

"Here, cover up with this," he said. He was almost frantic as he handed it to me.

We went through the toll booth, then he turned the car around and doubled back heading to Glen Oaks. He drove to the train station at Woodside Avenue in Queens, parked the car, got out and opened the trunk. He came around to my side and handed me something that looked like a raincoat. I put it on and without a word walked into the train station.

GOD KEPT HIS WATCHFUL eye on me that night. I had only taken my third step up the landing leading to the platform, when the men in blue found what they had come looking for. They approached without hesitation in sure steps and joined me on either side, left and right. There was this odd sort of communication with them. They didn't speak to me but assisted in silence like they understood me completely. They didn't question me or look in a pocket. They didn't hold my arm or touch me in any way. They simply walked next to me and escorted me to a police car.

I felt like I had gone through a war, but I was safe now that the men in blue had found me. There was a sense of comfort from the images of uniform and badge. It was a matter of minutes before I was back at Hillside Hospital.

There was nothing I could do then. They put me on the second floor, the locked unit. They didn't understand what happened and I couldn't find the words to tell them what happened, because my brain had disconnected itself from the part of my face that did the talking. All I could do now was wait and hope that my son was OK. I grew smaller inside somehow. Then I touched the anger.

It came seeping into my consciousness in a quiet but strong way. It began in a low place, visceral it was, from deep inside a primordial memory. Ancient instincts surfaced—old memories from far back in time, before the cradle of this humanity. Before human language. Before the blueprints of consciousness evolved themselves into the constructs of ideational imagery. Salt water and rock, slime and mucky muck, there was a hideous sense—a presence unnameable, from the darkest points of Neptune's world. Salt water memory settled in my ears, it flowed like blood and burned inside. The scent of dark blue—green—black formed my vision. There was no light there, only an inner perception of another time in this prison body cage of

138

eternity and beyond. I was salt water and rock—fish-woman—reptilian by name, giving birth to her own necessity, to her own racial memory. This was my burden. There was no place to escape to.

I bridled my anger, like a smoldering fire and kept it within me in good control, but I don't know how I kept it that way. It took two days for my speech to return. Then I found out that the night I escaped from Hillside was the same night my son slipped in the shower and hit his head on the edge of the tub, resulting in a serious injury that required his being hospitalized.

TWO MEN SAT IN the lunch room. They were therapy aides—I think that's what they were called. They had a newspaper spread out in front of them and the big guy with the sardonic smile was rattling off names. I can't remember them now, but they were the usual ones given to those graceful animals that fly like the wind—thoroughbred race horses.

I sat there quietly listening to both of them trying to pick the next sure thing. "Bet on Davona Dale," I said in a matter of fact way. I don't know why I liked that name, there was just something about it that appealed to me.

The big guy flashed me a you - don't - expect - me - to -

listen - to - you - do - you? kind of smile and put his nose back in the sheets.

I wasn't insulted. After all, why would anyone listen to a crazy woman like me? I just sat there for a while staring at the empty wall in front of me.

I really felt like smoking. I had managed to quit the damn things when I started school, but now sitting in the lunch room in a hospital for crazies, well, it just seemed like the thing to do.

I got up and walked down the hall to the music lounge. When I opened the door a cloud of smoke hit me in the face. The music was loud. I think it was The Moody Blues—one of my favorites back then. Patients sat there captivated by the dance of sound and smoke, cigarettes hanging from their lips.

Two women were fighting over the next pick for the turntable. One fellow claimed the whole couch for his own. His smelly dirty body was sprawled out over the length of the couch making it impossible for anyone else to sit there, as if anyone would.

A woman sat on the floor with her back to us looking at a magazine. I bummed a cigarette from her. I put it in my mouth and lit it, in one motion pulling the smoke deep into my lungs gaining a sense of control over something! Here I was for the second time in my life, with no control!

I was angry again, at myself this time, not like the last time when I was angry at everyone else. This time I was angry at me, for allowing this to happen. I hadn't learned, hadn't figured it out. I had to wonder then: was Allyson right? Was it hopeless? I had gotten by for six years without medication, but here I was again, worse then the last time for sure with shock treatments and those awful hideous memories of mucky muck, scaly slime. Good God! Where did it come from?

Why, why, why, ...why was this happening to me?

Why, why, why?

Why is a crooked letter, Mother used to say.

I WASN'T IN A dormitory this time, but a semi-private room that had pink walls. Pink is a soothing color, that's why it's used so often in crazy houses. Any muted pastel would do I suppose, but pink is popular somehow.

I sat in the room that was mine now, on an unfamiliar bed whose vinyl covering was awfully unfriendly and didn't hold a sheet too well. That bed was always a mess. No matter how I made the thing it never stayed neat.

The remnants of that primitive memory were haunting me. Memories of primordial fear-anger, of life lived in a form other than Homo-sapiens. It left powerful images in my mind connecting me to a part of myself I never knew existed, connecting me to another life form I could not name. This was something I couldn't begin to comprehend then... did not want to think about then... did not believe then... I just let those images go underground.

MY ROOMMATE HAD CANCER. She was twenty-five years old and married. She and herhusband had a two year old child, a beautiful little girl. I felt for her big time—and especially the kid. Hard to imagine how things like this can happen. Where is the sense of it all?

She cried a lot. My roommate I mean. I couldn't talk to her too much because she was very depressed and just beginning to deal with her feelings. Sometimes she was very withdrawn, but sometimes she would smile and then her beautiful face would light up. It really got to me

There are holes in my memory here, from the shock treatments I guess. I don't remember much of this hospitalization even though it was a three-month stint again. But there are a few things I can recall.

They put me back on those awful drugs and I went through the whole thing again with the side effects. There was nothing I could do about that while I was there, so I didn't worry about it this time.

Mother came to the hospital with the form so I could withdraw from classes at Hofstra and not get a bunch of F's for the term. It was like a terrible defeat then, having to bail out of a whole semester, but that was the way it was.

I don't remember my doctor's name or even seeing one the whole time I was at Hillside, but I know they have doctors there and I know I must have had one. I just don't remember who he was.

I SAT IN THE lunch room and those therapy aides were in there again. The big guy from the night before, the one with the smile was talking to his gambling partner, his co-worker. He looked at me kinda sideways out of the corner of his eye and said to his friend, "Know who took it in the third last night bro, that Davona Dale, son of a gun!" He slapped his knee and turned his head to look at me. I just sat there minding my own business.

They had the sheets out for another race. The big guy went down the list rattling off names, one by one. I heard a name I liked again. "Glorious Song," I said under my breath. As they turned their heads to look at me I got up and left the room.

The dining facilities at Hillside were kind of weird. The

building we took our meals in was across the campus—I guess I can call it a campus because people did study and do research there. All kinds of people walked around real fast to show everyone how busy they were and how they could hardly keep up with themselves.

The food really was good there. One of the patients told me how people always tried to get into Hillside because of that great food, and besides you could eat as much as you wanted.

Hillside was light years ahead of Pilgrim. They were learning a lot about how the brain worked. They still couldn't figure out what was the matter with me though. They still treated me with those awful drugs.

Doctor no name ordered an EEG for me. I think it was to make sure I didn't have a brain tumor or something like that. I remember reclining in this chair. It was comfortable. My feet were stretched out and elevated, sort of like when you go to the dentist.

This lady technician with blonde hair and white freckled skin was putting this awful disgusting gel all over my head. It was cold I remember that. Then she stuck these little pancake things with wires everywhere, all over my scalp, the whole time talking to me telling me to relax, not to worry.

"Now close your eyes, take a deep breath." She was

fussing around at the machine, flipping switches and turning dials. I felt weird, but I wasn't too afraid. Then came the dream images.

I saw in my mind's eye fiery red mountains of gas swirling around, alive with mystery and intrigue. I saw chess pieces floating in a primordial soup, mixing with images of kings and queens. Dark, it was dark red-black-purple and blue melding together forming mountains of fire. It was another galaxy, another universe. No fear—there was no fear—only awe and respect for these images of kings and queens long gone to some other realm, some other dimension. They lay there in their quiet dignity, asking nothing, receiving nothing. I felt sad for them.

The sequence of images kept repeating, again and again, until the technician turned off the machine. Then the dream ended. I went back to my scheduled activities wondering if maybe now Doctor No Name might be able to figure out what was the matter with me.

IT WAS EVENING when I walked into the lunch room. Those two therapy aides with the racing sheets were in there again. They watched me until I sat down, then the big guy started talking.

"Well, bro, guess who pulled out the long shot in the fifth

last time? That's right man! Glorious Song did it!" They
were staring at me.

The big guy held the racing sheets under his nose, rattling
off names one by one. Each time he said a name he paused,
waiting to see if I would say anything. He went down the
whole list. I listened to every name he rattled off and then
without a word got up and left the room.

I REMEMBER LITTLE else here but the anger— how deep
it was, how powerful but quiet it was. I projected it outward
and kept people away from me. I needed to be left to myself,
to my loneliness. I did feel so alone then.

I was certain I belonged not to the green earth but to the
sea. Its darkness, its frigid unfriendliness was my heritage.
The light does not penetrate there and so my soul slept in
the darkness of that place.

I was discharged in May and invited to become part of a
research project on side effects. I did that for a while,
traveling back and forth to Hillside on the bus.

I remember sitting in this guy's office with my eyes
closed trying to touch my fingers to the tip of my nose, or
trying to clap my hands together with my mouth stuck open
like a moron. Weird stuff like that. I don't know if I contrib-
uted anything to science because I got tired of going back

and forth to the hospital on the bus week after week and dropped out.

My first thoughts after discharge were about returning immediately to school, but I was late for summer registration and I had my old pal back, Quasimodo. I couldn't take him to school with me. So I began to wean myself from those awful drugs for a second time.

It didn't take me nearly as long this time because I knew more by then. I knew how important sleep is and about good food and positive thinking. But most importantly, I was learning that I could control my own medication, which I would find out in the years to come was the key to staying out of hospitals. I started going to support groups and working out at a gym. I went back to school full time the following September.

Life returned to normal much quicker this time than the first. My enthusiasm for school returned. My love of learning brought me back to myself and life became more joyful. It was in May of 1981 that I made plans to attend the honors convocation at Hofstra.

I WAS ONLY A LITTLE bit upset about my grade point average which should have been 3.7 but wasn't. It was 3.67 because Hofstra took away all my pluses from Nassau when

I transferred.

Hofstra did that because they didn't have a plus-minus system when I began the term there. I understood that. But when they started using that system while I was enrolled there, I went to the Dean's office to see about getting my pluses back on my transfer credits from Nassau Community College, but they wouldn't do it. I felt sort of cheated. I guess that's why I did what I did at my graduation ceremony.

I remember that day quite well, how I embarrassed myself and my poor mother—not like my graduation from Nassau when she was so proud of me for receiving the academic area award.

Well anyway, I should have realized something was going wrong that day when I wanted to wear this beautiful antique white peignoir instead of my cap and gown. I thought I was a princess and princesses never wear black! How awful! I wanted to wear this wonderful princess outfit. I simply felt like a princess. I had read the story about that young girl who slept on all those mattresses and who had such sensitive skin she could feel a pea all the way through. I must have been stuck in the memory of the story of The Princess And The Pea, that morning.

I remember the day of my graduation the sky was beautifully sunny and gorgeous. All over the campus, red and white azaleas in full bloom stood out against patches of thick green grass. Splashes of yellow flowers lined the walkways, and willowy limbed cherry trees ripe with delicate pink blossoms danced in the gentle afternoon breeze.

Outside the Adams Crawford Playhouse, people were mulling around in anticipation. An usher came and lined us up and somehow I managed to get in the very beginning of the line. Well, at least it seemed like the beginning of the line.

The procession into the building took fifteen minutes. One by one, seats were filled with graduates. While I waited I searched the crowd hoping to see Mother but saw only a sea of unfamilliar faces.

A few moments later the officiating members of the ceremony paraded themselves out onto the stage in silence. They were dressed in these funny outfits from the middle ages, with long shiny robes trimmed in green or gold, and peculiar headpieces with matching scarves. Some had puffy sleeves tucked and rolled into braided bands at the elbows. One member carried a scepter.

I watched them walk across the stage in their strange attire not thinking much about the way they were dressed, until the last member of the group came into view.

149

I looked at the figure walking across the stage in front of me. Every time he took a step I blinked in disbelief. What was he doing here? Why was King Henry VIII walking out onto the stage? How did he get into my graduation ceremony I wondered? But then, I remembered how I had felt that morning. Well, I was so upset. I realized all of a sudden that I should have done what I wanted to that day when I was getting dressed—I should have worn the peignoir!

After a few moments someone began with the usual boring litany of graduation ceremonies and it was not too long before we were ushered up to the stage to receive our mock diplomas.

We were each given 3x5 inch index cards to write underneath our names the honors award we were to receive. I remember standing there with shaking hands trying to write clearly in spite of the fine hand tremors I fought against whenever I got nervous.

Well, I did not write Cum Laude, or Summa Cum Laude, or Magna Cum Laude, but what I did write in shameless letters clearly and legibly on my index card were the words All Three!—meaning, of course, I thought I should graduate with all three honors. And when the facilitator of this part of the ceremony called out my name and then the words "All three!" I walked casually across the stage and shook the hand of the man handing out the little scrolls. I returned to my seat in the front of the auditorium oblivious of what I had just done. But the worst wasn't over yet.

After all the graduates had received their little scrolls and everyone was seated for the last part of the ceremony I remember looking up at the stage and seeing there an unbelievable sight! What indignation I felt! That man dressed like King Henry had lost all his clothes! He was sitting there in my graduation ceremony bare naked, sitting there on a folding chair, with black-socked ankles, hairy legs sticking out—no dignity, no pomp and circumstance. I couldn't believe it! I was so insulted I got up from my seat, marched right up the center aisle of the Adams Crawford Playhouse and out the door.

Well, I guess I must have gotten stuck in the memory of the story of The Emperor's New Clothes, during the ceremony.

Mother said we couldn't go back the next day for the second half because they might try to take back my diploma. Besides, I was cycling into a manic episode and had to get a handle on the energy in a hurry before I wound up down the rabbit hole for a third time.

A great doctor helped out then. I went back on medication just in time before the energy got too strong, before my personality went underground. Even though I was dead set against using medication, I was beginning to see how important it can be in managing this powerful energy. And those circuits were beginning to burn in. Those new connections in my brain were starting to process. Connections between the primitive brain and the modern brain. That's what mania is I think—burn in—just like an electronic circuit.

I HAD ESCAPED MANIA this time because I went for help in time. Because I recognized the signs—loss of sleep and an increase in energy—I knew it was only a matter of days or maybe a week before the energy would take over my body and my mind. I would be unable to stop it if I waited too long. I would become helpless and out of control—a victim of a brain gone haywire and unable to process information properly. I knew it would happen, so I went for help. After about a month of taking major tranquilizers my sleep cycle re-established itself and I began to feel grounded. Then I was faced with a decision. For a third time in my life I had to decide whether I should stay on the medication prescribed for me or discontinue it. Once again, I chose to discontinue it for the same reasons I had in the past. Dr. Sears was the third doctor to diagnose me with Schizophrenia and she was the third doctor to prescribe major tranquilizers that made it impossible for me to function. I felt I had no choice.

I met my second husband standing in line in the Long Beach post office on Christmas Eve in 1980. We just got to talking about this and that in the most natural and comfortable way. We decided to have coffee together after we left the post office and one thing led to another, the way those things sometimes do, and that was the beginning of the happiest time of my life.

Daniel came from a world different from mine. His focus was completely practical and material. Running a business and making a financial success of it was his primary goal. He had a vending machine route and he was barely making ends meet working part time at it, but he was determined to see it grow, and become a financial success.

Our relationship blossomed around romance and work. I took over the office responsibilities and Dan concentrated on the service end. We went out together to find new customers, knocking on doors and speaking to people, leaving information about his small company everywhere we went. We were in a very fortunate position, but we didn't know it then, as the Long Island economy was on the edge of a tremendous growth cycle which made it almost impossible for us not to do well.

The next twelve years were happy and wonderful years.

Our business grew and it seemed our joint efforts pulling in the same direction brought nothing but good results. Dan is a person of boundless energy and determination. He is talented and practical and has a good business head. But as for me and my goals and my aspirations, they lay in a different direction and after some years they began to make themselves felt.

Dan could not understand the things I had been through with the manias. We were such different kinds of people, me with my head in the clouds and him with his feet planted firmly on the earth. Actually it's a wonder we did so well together for those years. But questions of the spirit will not go away. They must be answered sooner or later or one really will go mad. I needed to have those answers. I needed my world to make sense. I needed to find some people of like mind to sort it all out with. That's when I met Emily.

SHE HAD BLACK HAIR. Short straight black shiny hair with purple roots. She had big round Greek eyes that reminded me of olives, and pale skin that was anemic looking—too too white against her black hair and large olive-sized eyes.

She said she was a witch, but not a bad witch, she was a good witch—a wiccan, which is the real thing. Not like those Halloween types that fly around on broomsticks and dress in long black gowns. She said she was from the ancient order of witches that believed in doing good deeds and stuff like that. I was pleased to make Emily's acquaintance.

Now it's true she was a crazy woman, just fun loving in a reckless adolescent sort of way. But I liked her from the start so I never said anything about her behavior which could be outrageous at times—like meeting all kinds of strange people at bars and walking on the beach late at night with people she didn't know too well—or hitchhiking! Dear god she really was reckless! And I certainly would never do those things unless I was manic—which I guess Emily was all the time, only I didn't know it then because I still didn't know anything about bi-polar disorder, even after two hospitalizations and a bunch of different doctors. I knew Emily wasn't right though. She was like a speed freak most of the time, high energy and very impulsive, especially for a Virgo—they don't usually behave that way, you know.

It seems sort of appropriate that we met at Theresa Dixon's angel class. Theresa had a thing for angels and loved to teach whoever would come to her home to learn about strata and hierarchies of angelic beings, and about mysterious persons coming and going in the lives of people she had known. And that these people had to be angels— the coming and going people I mean, showing up at just the right time to intervene in a crisis, and stuff like that.

Theresa played the piano. Actually she was a piano teacher and she played the organ for the choir on Sundays too. She looked like someone who would play the organ in church with her short bob of a hair cut and freckles—who would believe at her age anyone could have freckles still? And her straight below the knee polyester skirts, all nice and neat looking with these immaculately white linen blouses, long sleeved at that and buttoned just so at the wrist and, oh yes, a ribbon tied under her chin in a little Gerber baby bow. She always wore Red Cross shoes too, beige Red Cross shoes.

Theresa kept a beagle under a piano in her living room. Well, that's where the dog stayed every time we met at Theresa's house, which was every Wednesday evening. And every time we met, the dog—his name was Sydney by the way—well, he would lie there and go 'yup' 'yup', and scratch at the fleas on his belly every time his mistress said the word "angel". Theresa told him over and over again to shut up but it didn't do any good.

Theresa and the dog would just continue on and on in a

kind of inane duet, Theresa saying the word "angel" all the time and that stupid dog 'yupping' and scratching his belly. Well we—meaning the group of ladies meeting there to learn about angels—we decided not to go to the second half of Theresa's angel class the following month, but to start our own group. And that was the end of that.

WE INVITED THIS PSYCHIC channeler to come to one of our Wednesday evening gatherings. He was sort of famous in a small way, locally I mean. But I believe he was genuine and besides he was pretty damn funny to listen to. I saw a colored light jump off his neck one time while he was standing in the middle of a room talking. No kidding. It was red though and I don't know what that means, but I never saw any other colors jump off his body.

This guy, I'll call him Albert. I can't tell you his real name of course, him being famous and all that, but anyway this guy Albert was very interested in a bunch of stars called the Pleiades. He was an expert on them and insisted he was from that place. He said I was from a place called Sirius and that was way I was so serious, which I suppose I am, but I really don't think I am from Sirius because I don't think any of that stuff is real. But I never told that to Albert.

We always had a lot of laughs when we got together and

the reason I think Albert the psychic was genuine and not a fake is, well, I have a good reason but I can't tell you. It's too private. But he told Emily all kinds of interesting things that made her very happy, like she was going to be making a lot of new friends in the coming months and that she was going to get to go back to school—she wanted to be a nurse—and that she was going to get to go to the witches' ball in Salem that year, and that she was going to see Arlo Guthrie sometime soon—he was her favorite singer, she said.

We did a lot of talking. We learned about different kinds of meditation too, with fancy lights and electronic sounds. And we all learned to make these funny breathing groaning noises to help us meditate better. I thought it was a lot simpler with a plain ordinary candle myself, but apparently simplicity has been replaced with ceremony these days.

Once we got into a conversation about the goal of the spiritual life. A frivolous discussion ensued about the merits of having fun and taking things lightly, as well as about the dangers of being too serious. I was the only one in our group of five ladies who was in disagreement with the prevailing mood of the day, believing a true path must be a sacred path or it must be a worthless path after all. I soon learned to keep my opinions to myself.

I was walking the road of dissatisfaction by then with

everything I had learned in life. Two bouts of mania and loads of unanswered questions were haunting me. What was the nature of the mind I wondered? Where does the "I" that I am exist? Inside my brain? Do I run my brain or does my brain run me? And if my brain is running me, then where does that leave me? After being catapulted into other dimensions these sorts of questions take on some importance.

Eastern mysticism soon became my focus and the concept of kundalini energy offered the best model to me for understanding what had taken place during my manias. In the literature I found common threads of experience that I could relate to. It was the best explanation I could find in a society that is totally unprepared to address seriously the effect of experiences of altered states of consciousness on an individual.

My mind was awash in questions, but there were never any answers. No one was available who could tell me what was going on for sure. I had to figure it out for myself, just like everyone else on the planet. The worst part of it all seemed to be that no one was willing to talk about things of the spirit and mental illness. What, I wondered, was everyone so afraid of?

I waded in with timid steps, uncertain that the grace of

God would carry me. What past ills had I committed that had produced this situation in my life?

I began to see very clearly then that the purpose and the point of it all was not about establishing the credibility of my own ego as I had once thought. The point of it all was learning about trust. Learning to cultivate total and complete trust in His grace. And learning that each one of us carries a spark of divinity within, and it is forever untainted and undefeated. No matter what happened along the way I had to trust Him.

THE DEMON RETURNED ONCE more in 1991. It came without warning, without provocation. It sneaked into my life quickly this time, and I was so busy with my everyday affairs I didn't see it taking shape, I didn't see it rearing its ugly head. Ten years had passed since my last episode of mania. I had forgotten what I learned back then. I had forgotten there was a force to contend with in my life.

I started to miss sleep but I was too busy to pay attention. I started to lose weight but wasn't making any connection between the signs. I still had no formula to apply to my situation so that I could recognize what was happening. I still didn't know that it was the beginning of mania. It just seemed like I wasn't sleeping too well and had lost a pound or two.

I remember walking into my bedroom one afternoon and finding the entire contents of the closet scattered across the floor. Boxes of books, dirty laundry, coat hangers, shoes and sneakers, a vacuum cleaner and God knows what else was all over the room. I stopped short and looked at the mess in disbelief, wondering who had emptied the closet out like that. I was the only one in the house.

Returning to the room an hour later I was equally amazed to see all was back in place, and once again I stopped short, and wondered in disbelief, who had done it? How had it happened when I was the only one in the house?

My husband Dan began to notice something was wrong with me. He took me to our family doctor, who examined me and shook his head not knowing what to say except to direct him to a shrink. We went to see Dr. Havalin.

I remember sitting in his office staring with wide eyes at all the photographs on the walls of the room, saying nothing at all. The shrink sent me across the street to a medical hospital believing my condition was caused by some "toxic" substance in my body.

It was while I waited in the emergency room with Dan that the mania swallowed up my ego whole and took complete control.

I WAS ON A SPACE SHIP. I was lying on a sterile table wearing a peculiar cloth gown with funny little bumpy dots all over it. I had no shoes on and my feet were cold. The lights above me were glaring, bright and buzzing. I had never heard lights buzzing before. I watched technicians fussing around at the control center in the spaceship. They were all very busy checking this and that and running back and forth here and there. They had funny long coats and odd paper jackets over their shoes. They all wore green except the ones sitting at the control station. They wore white.

The air was tense with their busyness, with their technology. They all had their places to move in. Each knew his station. Everything progressed in clockwork fashion. They were efficient. They were in control.

Dan was gone. How long had I been there?

I watched the flurry of activity in front of me. I didn't question being on board the craft knowing that it was my very presence that was driving its journey. It was my mind, my mind that was to blame, for doing all of it, for putting all those people there like that, for making them look so busy. I knew I was doing it, but why?

They were speaking louder and louder up at the front, up at the control center. They were in a hurry, something was wrong. Tables were being moved about quickly, quickly, everyone was rushing.

I heard voices nearby. It was a language I did not recognize at first, but then it was suddenly familiar. My mind railed at the sound of it. Fear clamped down on my heart. The words they were speaking were German words... German words... German words....

Fear and memory washed over me. There was a girl— there was a memory of a girl. She was strapped down on a gurney, she was screaming. Legs and arms flew about and then she was quiet. I remembered her in that moment, how she was quiet after they did it to her.

One day became the next.

Something had happened again. There was a familiar discomfort. I had felt it before, yes, when I came to and Mother was there. The boundaries of time split open, and I was transported to another place, to another dimension. My heart was pounding, pounding, pounding ...

I lay there telling my heart to be silent, trying to slow the fury of its beating, trying to stop the rhythm of breath that issued the final measure of my life in obscene gasps and starts for air. It was so loud I knew they would find me.

Four points of restriction described my prison of terror, now that I could hear the voices again. Those words, those words, were coming at me...

It seemed as if days passed while I remained on the table. I did not grow tired or hungry from the screaming. Always the voices were there in the distance and they would come and I would scream more.

It's the memory of these things....the memory of these things...the memory...

I entered the soft cocoon of my body, into the place called mind and awareness. Pulling together the parts, sensing the energies five layers deep—the nightmare was over. It was safe to return.

I opened my eyes. It was dark. I was in an unfamiliar room. There was no sound, no movement around me. I could barely make out the shapes and forms on the table at my bedside. I could dimly see a vase of roses, some get well cards and someone was sitting there. It was Dan. He was concerned, and understanding and loving. "I heard you were giving the nurses a hard time yesterday, what was all that carrying on about?" He held my hand and smiled in a gentle way. There were no words to tell him what had happened.

I walked the hallway later while the nurses looked on in an amazed way at the transformation that had taken place within forty-eight hours. I had gone from a screaming insane human being to a perfectly lucid and rational individual.

The intervention had been two injections of Thorazine.

I was discharged after four days and instructed to return to Dr. Havalin for follow up. His assessment of the situation was that I had been overcome by a "toxic" substance and he did not see the need for further medical treatment.

Still I had no clue as to what had been happening to me. There was no way to explain or account for these temporary shifts in my personality. No way to explain where they came from, or why they came at all. Seventeen years had gone by and I was still clueless.

I dug deeper into the world of metaphysics looking for some answers. Always I would come back to the theories on kundalini energy. There was no model available that I could find in a Western approach; the only information I could find was embodied in the teaching of the East. And what I was learning there was that what I had been suffering with was simply a disruption and lack of control in a field of energy. It was the brain, not the mind that was at fault, but only the brain. A transducer of energies of sight and sound and smell and touch and taste that would at times lose its ability to transduce properly and simply mix up its fields. Put them in the wrong place so to speak. Sort of like trying to see with your ears or taste with your eyes. It was a case of mechanical failure. Fields of memory and fields of time meshed and blended together, until I was swallowed whole by my own subconscious.

I started to think more and more of my body as a machine and to see clearly that the "I" that exists is separate from the body. The "I" that is my true self originates from spirit not from matter. There was a distinction that had to be made between these two. What had to be kept clear in my mind was that "I", originating from spirit, cannot dominate matter—matter is a formidable opponent. Only God can dominate matter and I am not God. I was always wanting to fix it, fix me, to not have this condition whatever it was after all, I simply did not know and did not care to have it. Like a giant puzzle things came together, piece by piece, memory by memory, impression by impression.

I became serious about the practice of meditation. I believed that if I could learn to have better control internally it would help me gain some measure of control over what had been happening to my body. I would discover later this was an absolutely false premise. Always I wanted to believe that the locus of control was in my hands, when always it is in God's. There was no power within my grasp that could prevent or change the course and nature of this energy except to be found by taking medication. It would not be until a few years later that I would come to fully understand this.

Months passed by and once again after the disruption of a major episode, life settled into a familiar pattern.

I continued with Emily and the ladies on Wednesday evenings, but grew less and less interested in social gatherings of this kind as I was becoming more serious about the study of metaphysics. I began to resent such a carefree and frivolous approach to what was becoming sacred to me. I simply didn't like the atmosphere.

I needed to know who I was. I needed to know that I was not "crazy". I needed to believe that my internal experiences had value, even if they were not understood by the people around me. I needed to believe that God would love me and accept me even if at times I entered into states of mind that were beyond my own comprehension. Perhaps at times I was possessed by the dark force. Certainly at least, being without control in that way it is just the same. But I had to believe that I was still one of His beloved children, and could find my way to His Grace if I did not give up hope.

Finally, nine months later, in the midst of my fourth mania, God sent into my life a man who would change it forever. He sent me Dr. Saba.

IT BEGAN IN FLORIDA the fourth time, this bout with the demon that was to become the blessing in disguise that would finally change my life. It was Christmas time and I had stayed too long after Dan returned to New York. I should not have stayed but for my mother I did. She was ill and in need of help. Her health and well being had been declining. Slowly she had lost herself in an unhappy marriage. Her husband was a terribly overbearing and selfish little man who could only think of his own needs, someone who could not bear the thought of losing his wife to divorce and so had been trying to convince her to stay by using tactics of guilt and pleading and carrying on like a little child. Slowly my mother's spirit was being beaten and it was during that holiday season that she first sought treatment for depression.

The health professionals caring for Mother agreed that it would be in her best interest not to remain in the home she shared with her husband. The only option that I could see was to stay in Florida and wait until she was well enough to travel so that she could return with me to New York. I did not consider that I was overstepping my bounds or interfering in their marriage. I did not imagine that I was doing anything other than what I absolutely had to. I was certain that my mother had to return with me to New York or she would never be well.

While I waited for the days to pass I began losing sleep. I was in trouble. I knew I should have returned to New York, that I might be taking a risk I could not afford to take, but I couldn't leave her there.

On January 2, Mother said she felt well enough to travel. The next day we were packing the van to leave. We made sandwiches, remembered bottled water, took a map, and said our prayers while we pulled out of the driveway. I had missed two nights of sleep by then, but I felt just fine. I remember thinking how late it was to start off that morning. It was already ten o'clock as we headed across route 50 on our way to the interstate highway. Everything went well until we drove through Ocala.

There was something peculiar about the signs. We were headed north but the signs said we were going south. My sense of direction, usually so acute, was completely gone. It was as if I was driving from a point of center that moved in all directions with my attention. There was no time or space or distance to travel. If we stayed perfectly still the rotation of the earth would simply bring our destination to us. The laws of gravity had ceased to operate. Mother looked at the map while I drove into the unknown.

I loved driving my van. It gave me a real sense of control.

Being on the road in a thing like that, well you just knew you were serious about going someplace, and I was serious about going someplace. I just didn't know where I was going. And as strange as it may sound it was not important at the time, it was only important that we go somewhere.

Mother squinted at the map, wrinkling her forehead as she tried to trace the path of our journey in pencil. "Pull over please sweetie, will you? Maybe I can figure out what's going on here. It looks like we're going in the right direction but I can't make this out."

I began looking for a place to pull over, and noticed that the landscape had changed. It all looked so absolutely charming. Tall oaks thick with Spanish moss lined the highway, creating deeply shaded restful spots for masses of pink and white wildflowers. The embankment was covered with a thick layer of grass that was a deep dark green—I had never seen such a shade of green. We were in horse country now and passing by one after the next, stable after stable, where any number of champion thoroughbreds might be resting up for the next Kentucky Derby. The magic of horses was in the air. The thrill of their beautiful carriage, their grace, their dignity, their wonder could be felt as we drove along that highway.

Passing by a cottage I remember thinking to myself that

171

it looked as if it belonged in a fairy tale. Suddenly Mother blurted out, "There! Stop! Let's ask someone!" She pointed her finger in earnest at the fairy tale cottage.

I pulled the van over to the side of the road. We got out and walked over to the door of the cottage— it was such a pretty place. My heart sank when I read the sign on the door: TAXIDERMIST it said. I tried to peek inside the windows to see if there were any poor old thoroughbreds hanging around waiting to get stuffed. I didn't see any of those or anything else for that matter. The place gave me the creeps. I felt relieved when no one answered Mother's knocking and we continued on our way.

Back in the van Mother studied the map some more. I ate a peanut butter and jelly sandwich, while Mother finished looking and announced we were going in the right direction so we should just continue.

Mother put the map back in its compartment, grabbed herself her own peanut butter and jelly sandwich, buckled her seat belt and said, "Let's rock and roll baby." I had never heard Mother talk like that, sort of slang as it was, and I thought she was loosening up a bit and that seemed like a good thing to me and I was happy about it as we drove off again into the unknown.

Ten minutes later Mother started talking to me about

Indians.

"Chief Osceola laid down his life here," Mother said. She seemed to be lost in some kind of internal remembrance of the Chief. "He took his people into the swamps because the soldiers couldn't follow them there." Her reverie continued as she stared out the window. Her face looked blank and sorrowful. "All those brave Indians just walked into the swamps, just like that. Can you imagine such a thing?"

I was afraid she was starting to have a nervous breakdown. I was not used to hearing Mother say such strange things. Suddenly I was thinking about Indians myself. About the terror and the tragedy of their people. About the shame of the White Man, and the injustices he had committed against Native Americans. I could hear the earth crying for its loss. I was suddenly caught up in the emotion of it all, of its awful bloody history. I felt like crying. Even the magic of Ocala couldn't make me feel better.

Thirty minutes passed and the signs were telling me we were going south. Once again we had to stop the van and check the map. What was going on? It was like a bad dream, a circular bad dream and we would be forever lost in Ocala with the magic of the horses and the sorrow of the Indians and we would never find our way to New York.

By the grace of God we got into Georgia at eight o'clock

that night. What should have taken four and one half hours took us ten and Mother decided she'd had enough of my driving around in circles. We needed a room for the night and a telephone so she could call her brother to come and rescue us. That was the night we stayed at The King's Inn.

I WANTED MY OWN ROOM. I didn't want to share a room with my mother. I don't know why, why I was being so difficult. I simply needed to rest. I was so tired by then I needed my own space. Mother didn't argue, and the man at the desk was quite obliging of course. "We'll take good care of you ma'am. Two rooms? Of course, no problem! Do you need wake-up service? Ice is at the end of the hall to your left. Is there anything I can do for you? Call New York? Why of course—right here's the phone." He had cardboard hair that stuck up into the air two inches over his head and tiny black eyes that darted back and forth in a nervous sort of way. He didn't look too good to me.

I went to my room. It was pretty big, probably big enough for three or four people—two double beds and all that. Well, I felt kind of bad about getting my own room then, but I really needed to be alone for a while. Everything in the room was red. The carpet and the wallpaper and the bedspread and everything was all kingly looking—it being

The King's Inn of course it had to have a kind of royal appeal.

I tried to take a nap. It was almost ten o'clock and since I couldn't sleep I decided to take a walk, which wasn't a bad idea, except I still had no sense of direction and went out into the Georgia night and got lost.

Well, I really don't care about going into it, how I got picked up by the police and how they took me to the hospital and how my poor tired mother had to come and get me. She had notified the police that I went out walking and disappeared so after they found me and figured out who I was, they actually called her—can you imagine? They were really special people.

Well, the next day, my uncle and my husband flew into the closest airport, took a cab to The King's Inn and the four of us proceeded to make our way to New York.

Dan drove while Mother sat in the front, and I sat in the back next to my uncle. I looked out the window and watched the world going by: images in kaleidoscope, streams of light, streaks of color, trees, fields of corn, fields of corn, cows in pasture, horses.

Old memories and ideas began to move inside my head with the images in my view. I remembered the diamond mines. There was a time when my family owned diamond mines. I was a princess then, and Mother was a queen. There was a time, yes, there was a time when we lived like that.

I watched out the window and saw there on the ground the astral bodies of dead animals that had died on the side of the road after being hit by cars. There were dogs, cats, squirrels, armadillos, possums, even deer, some larger and unidentifiable shadows of life forms, their energy fields still remaining so long after the disintegration of their dense bodies. I didn't know how I could see such a thing as that with my eyes but they were there clearly and sadly, and my heart filled with sadness from their pain. The world moves too fast to care, they are only animals after all.

That night we stayed somewhere, but I cannot say where it was. I was lost deep into the mania. Lost beyond the boundaries of my familiar world.

The next night I remember pulling into the driveway at my uncle's house in Valley Stream on Long Island. We all went into the house for a cup of coffee. Mother stayed in Valley Stream. Dan and I drove home to Bayshore.

As I lay awake in bed, at three o'clock in the morning beyond the reach of sleep and gazing at the ceiling, there came into my view the most extraordinary sight! From the window on the north wall of the room, an entity entered my world. Its form was composed of a beautiful pale green light and was surrounded by a kind of energy of love. There is no way to explain this, but somehow this light being was communicating the most extraordinary emotion of love! My heart stilled, and my breath became suspended as I watched this most beautiful creature in such a playful and happy way become the shape of a flute and fly across my room to the opposite wall. There it settled itself onto the glass, covering a photograph of a giant panda with her baby. It rested there only a moment before crossing back to the opposite wall and disappearing from my world through the window.

It left me breathless and filled with joy that there could exist somewhere such an entity as this! What wonder there was in the world! I didn't know it in that moment when I first saw it, but I came to understand later on that it had been a harbinger, a messenger of things to come in my life, for it was the very next day that I would finally meet the person who would help transform my life, the person who would help me begin to make sense of it all. I was finally going to meet Dr. Saba.

FOR THE SECOND TIME Dan was faced with a manic wife. He knew our family doctor couldn't help so he called Dr. Havalin, the doctor that helped out nine months earlier. He told Dan to take me to Southside Hospital, and that there

I could be cared for. Southside had one floor dedicated to psych, a small unit of just twenty beds, a nice and relatively quiet environment.

It was the morning of the next day when my world was changed forever, the day I first met Dr. Saba. He walked into my room and his presence filled every cubic inch of space, like a light filling in the cracks of darkness. There are no words that can accurately describe the impression that this man made on me. There are things that pass between people—silent things, sacred things that cannot be described by our human language. These are things of the spirit. We have all felt them and when we have the good fortune to encounter them, then we are blessed.

I gazed in amazement at the tall distinguished looking Indian doctor standing before me. His carriage, his demeanor, his vibration, spoke of ancient Aryan wisdom. That this man was descended from royalty was obvious to me and I wanted to bow at his feet. It was a reaction that I cannot explain and could not comprehend at the time, but I knew instinctively that this was no ordinary doctor.

He stopped two feet from my bed, looked directly into my eyes and said, "Hello, I am Dr. Saba, how are you feeling?"

I was immediately captivated by the sound of his voice,

by his friendliness, by his genuine concern. My heart was filled with joy, and for the very first time in my experience with the madness that plagued my life, I believed things would finally begin to get better. God had sent me a doctor who would truly help me. He had sent me a doctor who could help me understand what had been happening to me. He had sent me a guru.

Dr. Saba ordered an EEG, blood tests, medication for the mania. He saw me every day during the two weeks I stayed at Southside Hospital. I had very little to say to Dr. Saba during those initial visits. I always became tongue-tied in his presence, always feeling as if I needed to bow or make myself very small when he entered the room, always cognizant of who he was, not just an ordinary doctor, but who he really was in the larger scheme of God's plan, which I understood even then as something we all take part in, if only we can see it.

The first time I visited Dr. Saba in his office after I had been discharged, he explained to me that I had manic-depression and he wanted to treat me with Lithium. He gave me literature to read about the drug. Dr. Saba explained that Lithium is not really like other drugs, it's a salt, something called lithium carbonate. It seemed sort of odd to me to think that a salt was going to help me, but if this doctor said it would then I believed it would. At least he didn't want to keep me on those awful drugs that would bring Quasimodo back again, drugs like Prolyxin or Thorazine.

I explained to Dr. Saba that I had taken Lithium in the past when I had been depressed and it didn't help me. Dr. Saba explained that Lithium is best suited to treat mania, not depression. Depression, he explained, should be treated with anti-depressants. I had been free of depression for fourteen years and had only been experiencing mania, so Lithium became a part of my life.

The second time I sat in Dr. Saba's office I noticed on his desk a beautiful monogrammed name plate. It sat there staring at me, demanding that I notice it. Mithur Krishna it said. Mithur Krishna? Mithur Krishna? His middle name was Krishna! Suddenly in a flash of insight the visitation of the entity only three weeks before made sense! That beautiful pale green light, that magical joyful creature that came into my bedroom at three in the morning had been a harbinger of things to come. The flute made sense then—there was the connection! It was announcing Dr. Saba in a playful way, the only way I could understand because Dr. Saba's middle name was Krishna! Can there be any question that God talks to us in the most extraordinary ways, and that in the case of someone as dense as I am He has to get pretty darn specific!

Sometimes when I sat in Dr. Saba's office I was entertained by his chair. On more than one occasion his armchair, which appeared to be an ordinary arm-chair the kind any doctor might have beside his desk, well this chair would begin to go ding, ding, ding, ding! It sort of sounded like there was a winner at a slot machine in the room with us. The first time this happened I figured it was my imagination. The second time I knew it wasn't and looked at Dr. Saba expecting him to explain the meaning of this strange event, but he just kept on with what he was doing. I never did figure out how that chair behaved like that.

After seeing Dr. Saba for about twelve months and learning the basics of manic-depression, I was feeling anxious about asking the big questions. I wanted to talk about the real stuff inside me. I wanted to get serious. I was afraid that if I started sharing the craziness of my manias with my doctor he would increase my medication and send me for psychotherapy. I knew he came from India, but he was trained in Western medicine after all.

One day I drummed up the courage to begin to share what was really bugging me. "Dr. Saba," I said, "when I get manic I remember all my past lives."

He looked at me directly and in the most serious way said

to me, "You must learn how to communicate so the next time you meet people on the path they will understand you."

It was as if someone slapped me in the face. He didn't reach for the prescription pad. He didn't question or ask me to explain. He understood what I was saying. He understood completely and there had opened up a dialogue between doctor and patient that was the beginning of healing, a dialogue that was wonderful and rare within the confines of Western psychiatry.

I spent three short years with Dr. Saba and received an education in the management of manic-depression and of the understanding of spirit. I came to understand through my doctor that our experiences of phenomena are of no consequence. Whether we have visions or not—whether we enter tunnels in meditation or not—whether we experience psychic phenomena or not—whether we experience mania or not—whether we remember past lives or not, these things are meaningless. These are distractions. They are the trappings of Maya. They are the dance. The dance with the serpent. The dance of the senses. I had always thought these were the hallmarks of spiritual growth. Dr. Saba taught me that is all nonsense. Spiritual growth has nothing to do with what is perceived with the sense mind. Sense mind is full of trickery. It fools us into believing false pictures on the screen of life. Every time I entered into mania, sense mind brought me to a new and different reality. Which one was real? My "normal" state or the psychotic one? The answer of course is neither one. Both are false. And here resides a great lesson. The lesson is that only intuition can teach us. We must close off our minds, go to the empty place, sit in the silence and listen with the ears of our soul. Then we may begin to learn.

Psychosis is a gift because it is a hard and fast teacher. Many people would never see it that way. But it is what I have learned. It is what makes sense to me. As I grew in self-love and acceptance of my illness and embraced it for what it could teach me, the essence of what I was to learn was revealed to me.

I finally understand a simple truth. So simple a child can understand. Spiritual growth is measured by our increasing capacity for love, not our increasing capacity to reason things out through the intellect. St. Augustine had much to do with the evolution of thought in Western culture. He was able to reason his way to a higher state. Most of us will find the way of love a more certain and faster path.

In my case I had to come to total self-love and acceptance to override the burden of mental illness. I was able to do that because I had the good fortune to meet a doctor who was able to help me make sense of things and to grow in the abundance of love. This is an example of how God works in our lives if we are receptive to Him.

On a clear crisp early winter day in 1994, I was in the garage sorting through some boxes of old clothes preparing for our annual trip to Florida, the one Dan and David and I make every Christmas to be with our mothers. I came across a jacket that had been packed away and forgotten for many years. As I absent-mindedly checked the pockets, I was surprised to find a small object nestled in one of them. Curious fingers lifted it from its hiding spot. Memories and emotions came flooding back to me as I looked at it remembering who had given it to me and why. After so many years to be holding in my hand the little owl given to me by Kandi—the gift she had given me for good luck on my quest—well, it was like a small measure of closure. How ironic it was, I thought in that moment: all along I'd believed it was a quest for knowledge I'd been after. But it had never been about that at all. It was really a quest for love. It's very simple I understand now. Love has all the answers.

...*Sri Krishna with the enchanting melodies*

of his heavenly flute, calls all souls to the bower of Divine Love there to bask in blissful union with God.

God Talks with Arjuna: The Bhagavad Gita
Paramahansa Yogananda

EPILOGUE

It may seem odd to some people that an individual would choose to share a story such as the one contained in these pages. What is the purpose? What can the writer hope to accomplish one might ask? What benefit can there be to others from a story such as this?

The very same questions plagued me as I set the words down page after page. My mind turning this way and that, divided against itself, wanted to tell this story and wanted to not tell it at the same time.

For how does one communicate in human language with paper and ink that which is told to us in spirit? How can one explain from words anchored in the outer layers of mind the deeper whisperings of the soul that make all things right with the world? How does one describe a shift of attitude? Of perception? Of consciousness? Or the difference between how the light looks at six o'clock in the morning and at one minute after?

But this story is exactly about all of that. About how the light looks different at one minute past six. It is a story about a fundamental change. In attitude. In perception. In consciousness. It is about a change each one of us must make if we are to reach our goal. And that goal is God. Whether we admit it or not, that is the goal. It is the birthright and final destiny of every human soul.

The problem for those of us reared in a culture based on materialism and consumerism is formidable when we speak of a higher consciousness and spiritual matters. We are taught that seeing is believing, but things of the spirit cannot be seen in a physical sense. We move in the world seeking always outward things to entertain and enliven us, but spirit calls us inward to a place we have not yet learned to see.

It is a curious truth that a psychotic mind once restored to health has a distinct advantage in understanding. For it has surely learned that what is perceived in the material world cannot be true. A psychotic mind once restored to health has gained an understanding that is not easily attained. It knows that what is perceived with the sense mind, the material mind, is false. It has broken the chains of material-ism, or at the very least it has taken an important step in that direction. Of course this is still a matter of perception and of "seeing".

Health will not necessarily restore us to God. But God will always restore us to health. There is a difference of course. Health of the spirit brings full life on all levels. Health of the body if it does not extend to other planes, leaves a restriction in the life of the individual.

There are certain things most of us can do to keep ourselves healthy in body. We can exercise control over what we eat and exercise our physical forms. We can take medication if we have to and learn to be responsible for our own health. We have power here. More than we know until we begin to see it for ourselves.

I have experienced wonderful control and balanced energy from a regular program of walking. I have been walking for twelve years and know too well that if I do not walk I will not feel well.

I know too the power of food and that I will make myself mentally and spiritually sick if I eat incorrectly. Food has an intimate relationship with spirit. We have not learned to think of food in these terms but it's true. And I have learned finally, that my body will not function properly without medication. I resisted this idea for years thinking that because I took medication I was somehow spiritually unfit. But of course that came from ego. Spirit doesn't care if I take medication or not.

I have been blessed because in my case Lithium is a wonder drug. I need only a tiny amount to stay healthy and suffer no ill effects from it. Many people are not as fortunate.

Whether we know it or not, each one of us harbors the same heart's desire. To find peace. To reach a state of health in body, mind and soul. Layers of being superimposed one over another like transparent pieces of film. Light passes through the layers animating the very life of us. It is not the image on this film that matters, but that the light passing through may do its work.

My prayer for us all is for healing. May we become patient. And gentle. And kind. May we learn to grow in love for ourselves and for those who have wounded us. For it is in wounded relationships that the seeds of illness take root. It is here love meets its greatest challenge. In the dark places.

When we dance let it be a dance of joy. Why be troubled by illusion? Our lives are only images held within those layers of film. They are not real. Only the light passing through them is real. That is what we are. We are that light.

Suggestions for Further Reading

Andreasen, Nancy. *The Broken Brain: The Biological Revolution in Psychiatry.* New York: Harper & Row, 1984.

Bentov, Itzhak. *Stalking the Wild Pendulum.* New York: E. P. Dutton, 1977.

Bragdon, Emma. *The Call of Spiritual Emergency: From Personal Crisis to Personal Transformation.* San Fransisc, Calif.: Harper & Row, 1990.

Campbell, Joseph. *The Mythic Image.* Princeton, N.J.: Princeton University Press, 1974.

Castaneda, Carlos. *The Teachings of Don Juan: A Yaqui Way of Knowledge.* New York: Simon & Schuster, 1968.

—. *A Separate Reality: Further Conversations with Don Juan.* New York: Simon & Schuster, 1983.

Cousins, G. *Spiritual Nutrition and the Rainbow Diet.* San Rafael, Calif.: Cassandra Press, 1986.

Grof, S. *LSD Psychotherapy.* Pomona, Calif.: Hunter House, 1980.

Grof, S. & C. Grof. *The Stormy Search for Self.* Los Angeles: J. P. Tarcher, 1990.

Halifax, J. *Shamanic Voices.* New York: Crossroads, 1979.

Krishna, Gopi. *The Awakening of Kundalini.* New York: E.P. Dutton, 1975.

—. *Higher Consciousness.* New York: Julian Press, 1974.

—. *Kundalini, The Evolutionary Energy in Man.* Berkley, Calif.: Shambhala, 1970.

—. *The Riddle of Consciousness.* New York: Kundalini Research Foundation, 1976.

—. *The Biological Basis of Religion and Genius.* New York: Harper & Row, 1972.

Sanella, Lee. *Kundalini: Psychosis or Transcendence?* San Franscio, Calif.:H.S. Dakin, 1976.

Tart, Charles. *States of Consciousness.* New York: E.P. Dutton & Co., Inc., 1975

Wilber, Ken. *The Atman Project.* Wheaton, Ill. Theosophical Publishing House, 1980.

White, John., (ed.) *Kundalini: Evolution and Enlightenment.* New York: Paragon House, 1990.

Yogananda, Paramahansa. *God Talks with Arjuna: The Bhagavad Gita.* Los Angeles, Calif., Self-Realization Fellowship, 1995.

—. *Man's Eternal Quest.* Los Angeles, Calif., Self-Realization Fellowship, 1982.

Additional copies of DANCING WITH THE SERPENT may be purchased at your local bookstore, or by sending a check or money order for $14.50 (includes two dollars and fifty cents for sales tax and shipping) to:

WaterMark Publications
P.O. Box 3366
Spring Hill, Florida 34611-3366

✂ --

Please send me _____ copies of DANCING WITH THE SERPENT. I have enclosed $14.50 per copy. DO NOT SEND CASH.

NAME   _____

STREET_____

CITY   _____

STATE   _____

ZIP   _____

*Please allow two weeks for shipping.

If you or someone you know has had a spiritual healing from mental illness and would like to share your journey, WaterMark Publications may be interested in hearing from you. Please send a self-addressed stamped envelope for submission guidelines to:

Nancy Harris
WaterMark Publications
P.O. Box 3366
Spring Hill, Florida 34611-3366